MOUNT EVEREST

I0203639

RICHARD S BAILEY

ADAPTED FROM THE STORY BY

JIM MEIROSE

MONTAG

First Montag Press E-Book and Paperback Original Edition June 2017

Montag Press
ISBN: 978-1-940233-42-0
Cover photos © abigail2resident; shrimpo1967
Interior book design and jacket © 2017 Niall Gray
Editor & Managing Director — Charlie Franco

A Montag Press Book
www.montagpress.com
Montag Press
1066 47th Ave. Unit #9
Oakland CA 94601 USA

Printed & Digitally Originated in the United States of America
10 9 8 7 6 5 4 3 2 1

For the dedicated women in theatre around the world who search for challenging roles.

"Mount Everest" is an excursion into expressionism. The style and images of the play spring from the mind of the protagonist, Christine Zidar, a young woman recently confined to a mental institution since childhood and then suddenly released. Once out of the institution, we see the world through Christine's eyes; but Christine does not see the world around her as others do. She has the aid of her friend, Leandra, a mysterious alter ego.

Waiting at home is her mother, Thelma, a woman who has been unable to cope with day to day life since the death of her husband. She has become a helpless hoarder and her home is stuffed and overwhelmed with trash bags and cardboard boxes holding years upon years of accumulated miscellany. Except for Christine's room. Thelma has kept Christine's room in pristine condition, awaiting her daughter's return.

Once home, Christine learns that because of neighborhood complaints about the trash, the city government is in the process of condemning the house for a variety of health and safety violations. Christine realizes she needs money to deal with everything and at Leandra's urging, turns to prostitution. She quickly gathers a list of johns who see her regularly. Her mind shapes an alternate reality where people are not who they appear to be but are as genuine to her as everyday reality is to others. And while she tries, she is unable to effectively deal with the city's administrative processes to stop the condemnation of her home.

In their dilemma, Christine and Leandra imagine themselves on the slopes of Mt. Everest among the dead bodies of those who have failed to scale the peak and been condemned. The cold, icy slopes offer a stark, peaceful reality she has never known, but yearns for. While the city relentlessly grinds on in its preparation to destroy her home, Christine and Leandra scheme to undermine the process. Their schemes fail.

Relentlessly searching for a non-existent solution, Christine retreats into her fantasies, forming a world of possibilities that don't exist. As her images of reality fail to find a resolution to her predicament, she and Leandra disappear into the lifeless expanse of bodies trapped for an eternity on the freezing slopes of Everest.

Cast (In order of appearance)

Christine Zidar
Leandra
Thelma Zidar
Martin Zidar
Lewis
Mrs. Petersen
Mary
Ronald Tanady
Barber
Deputy Mayor
Mayor
Francis Serdon
Diana
Barry Einhardt
Process Server
Paramedic 1
Paramedic 2
Mack
Sheriff 1
Sheriff 2
Other voices: Woman Voice 1, Woman Voice 2

Numerous roles in "Mount Everest" can be performed by a single actor to make the production more practical by reducing the size of the cast.

Casting Suggestions

Cast the same actor as:

Barber/ Process Server/Barry Reinhardt

Tanady/Paramedic 2, Deputy Mayor

Serdon/Mayor/Sheriff 2

Mack/Paramedic 1

Mary/Diana

ACT I

Fade up on the house jammed with overwhelming piles of cardboard boxes and mounds of heavy duty trash bags. They fill the kitchen and are piled high throughout. Various areas of the stage that initially present themselves as covered in trash will also open to reveal walls of city offices.

A space is cleared around the kitchen table. On a higher level is Christine's bedroom, illuminated in a faint pink light.

The door swings open. A notice is pinned to it. Thelma leads Christine in and stands at the open door.

THELMA
Christine, welcome home.

Thelma smiles joyfully and hugs Christine lovingly. Christine steps back and looks into Thelma's eyes

CHRISTINE
Is this where I live?

Thelma pulls Christine into the kitchen. Christine stops to take in the sheer volume of garbage bags stacked everywhere.

THELMA
I've got your room all ready for you. Upstairs.

Christine sees the notice on the door and picks it off and reads.

CHRISTINE
This says they're coming to inspect. What are you going to do? How are you going to get this place cleaned?

THELMA (WHISPERING)

Nosy damned neighbors. It's the nosy goddamned neighbors' fault. To hell with the Zidars. They say! They've always said to hell with the Zidars.

CHRISTINE

Mom. Mom, they've got reason. If the trash wasn't spread across the front porch and in the yard, they'd never have complained. It doesn't matter now, you've got two weeks before the inspector comes. What are you going to do?

THELMA

Nothing! Your Father wouldn't let himself be pushed around like this. We've gotten notices before, we've always appealed,

CHRISTINE

But this one says final notice, one last final notice. Did the other ones ever say final notice?

THELMA

Final is meaningless. This is the United States. They can't just throw us out of our house in the United States. This is my house. All paid off too, paid off long ago! This was the most beautiful house in the neighborhood. That counts for something! This is my house. It's paid off and I got the deed, Christine, I got the goddamned deed, they can't kick me out.

CHRISTINE

The deed isn't a license to turn a house into a trash dump Mom. We can't blame the neighbors for complaining about the way you've let this place go. It looks like they've been abandoned for Christ's sake. What is all this stuff? What is in all these bags and boxes?

THELMA

Nothing. Never mind all that, I need to show you to your room.

Thelma takes Christine's bag and leads her through the trash bags to the staircase.

Up, go up.

> Lights fade up on Christine's room, casting a pink glow over everything. There is a dresser, the vanity and a large stuffed chair. Everything is clean and immaculate. The door to the left leads to a bathroom. They enter through the door to the right. A large window up center looks out on a trees and a far off grassy knoll. Christine's bed sitting. The outside of the left and right walls of the bedroom have numerous trash bags attached. These walls are hinged and can swing out, concealing the trash bags and boxes, presenting a white surface for projections when opened.

Thelma is bursting with pride as she opens the door and brings Christine into the room.

THELMA
This is your bedroom, Christine.

CHRISTINE
This room? This is for me?

> Thelma puts the bag in the closet.

THELMA
Here. I'll go now, you get some rest, then I'll help you unpack.

> Thelma leaves through the door to the right. Christine goes to the bed. She presses the mattress. She sits on the bed and bounces. Suddenly she gets up, strips off all her clothes and gets under the comforter.

> Bedroom lights fade out.

> A pastoral, grassy knoll is projected beyond the window. A projection of Martin, Christine's father, appears in the center window. It looks toward the window and then approaches.

Christine sleeps motionlessly in the bed covered. Her head is almost lost in the large white pillows and comforter. Leandra's voice is heard from offstage.

LEANDRA (OFFSTAGE)
Hey. Hey Christine.

> Christine does not respond.

> Martin's Projection appears to step up extremely close to the window. His eye fills up the window. It looks inside at Christine as she sleeps.

Leandra appears outside the window, in front of Martin's projection, wearing a long white nightgown.

LEANDRA
Christine. Christine! Hey Christine wake up! Wake up!

> Martin's Projection steps back, looks to each side and disappears to the left, leaving the pastoral knoll in view.

Leandra comes to the window and looks through at Christine. Christine is still. Leandra comes through the window and goes to the bed. She looks closely at Christine.

LEANDRA
Christine! Are you going to sleep your life away? Wake up!

> Christine still does not respond.

Christine! Wake up now! Wake up now!

Christine stirs in the bed. Leandra reaches over and shakes her.

Christine! Christine!

Christine opens her eyes, props herself up on one elbow, looks at Leandra, and falls back to the pillow.

CHRISTINE

I'm sick.

Leandra takes a step back.

LEANDRA

You are? What do you have? Can I catch it?

CHRISTINE

I don't think so.

LEANDRA

You've been lying here for too long. Let's take a walk.

Christine gets out of bed. She wears a long white nightgown that matches Leandra's. They leave the room.

Lights cross fade from the bedroom to the kitchen, piled high with boxes and bags of garbage but with room for the table where Thelma sits, the TV screen flickering reflected off her face.

Christine comes in and sits down. Unseen by Thelma, Leandra inspects the trash; smelling it, rubbing bits of bag, listening for the sound of insects. Thelma turns to Christine and smiles lovingly.

CHRISTINE

Mom, my room is wonderful. Thank you so much. Mom, I don't know what I'm supposed to do; how am I going to make money and live?

> THELMA

Oh, the lord will provide.

> Christine gets up and goes to the door, Leandra follows.

> CHRISTINE

The other houses on the block don't have garbage piled in the yard like ours.

> Thelma sits silently.

> CHRISTINE

You can smell our house two houses away.

> THELMA

I wish to God Martin was here, he'd have known what to do.

> CHRISTINE

Mom. Clean the damned place up, that will help.

> THELMA

I, I can't do that.

> CHRISTINE

Why not?

> THELMA (BEGINNING TO CRY)

Not without Martin. I need Martin to tell me.

> Christine pointed to a corner of the living room and narrowed her eyes.

> CHRISTINE

There, Martin's there.

> THELMA

I don't see anyone.

CHRISTINE

I do. Martin, will you help us today?

THELMA

Don't mock me Christine, it's wrong, stop it, just stop it!

The bedroom wall opens

CHRISTINE

But dead people can do things. I know that. I know that because,

Thelma claps her hands over her ears.

THELMA

Stop it! Stop saying that, stop talking like that!

Thelma slaps Christine across the face, Christine looks at her mother with great soft eyes and reaches out to her.

Projection of Christine's eyes looks down at Christine and Thelma.

CHRISTINE

Mom, Mom, come here.

They embrace in the kitchen surrounded by the bags of trash. Christine whispers into her mother's ear.

CHRISTINE

Mom, we'll hire somebody, we'll get somebody to clean the place out, how much time does the notice say we have?

THELMA

We have two weeks, and then an inspector will come and decide if we can live here anymore.

Projection of Christine's eye's fades out. Bedroom wall closes.

CHRISTINE

What do you mean, "Decide if we can live here anymore."

She lets go of Thelma

CHRISTINE

Mom, where's your phone book?

THELMA

Oh I don't know. Why?

CHRISTINE

I'm going to see who can come to clean out this house. What is it they say? Take the bull by the horns, is that what they say; yes, we got to take the damned bull by the horns! Now where's the damned phone book? Tell me now! Where?

THELMA

I don't know, it's buried here somewhere. I never call anybody anyway.

CHRISTINE

Well we're going to make a call right now – we don't have any time. Which room is it in? I swear to God, I will tear this house apart to find it, how can you not know where your damned phone book is?

THELMA

We can't clean up, not without Martin.

Thelma sinks into her unburied chair in the kitchen; wrings her hands and begins to sob.

CHRISTINE

Then what are we going to do, Mom? We have to do something.

Thelma bends forward and continues to sob. Christine desperately pulls trash bags aside searching for a phone book.

CHRISTINE

I'm not going back to that hospital! I want to keep my room!
What the hell will we do? We've got to do something.

Thelma changes the TV station,

The flicker pattern on her face changes.

Christine gets up from the table and goes downstage. Leandra follows.

CHRISTINE

I need to make money.

LEANDRA

You've got something men want, Christine. You know what it is. It's
not just in New York and places like that; there are lonely men who
need you right here in Nebraska. God gave it to you. Men want it.

CHRISTINE

But I,

LEANDRA

Never mind "but". You're obliged to use what God gave you.
Look. There's a man. You've got what he wants. Go on. Ask him.

Leandra lightly runs her finger down Christine's spine.
She nudges Christine toward Lewis, a large older man
with bushy grey hair.

Him. Go on. You'll see. Ask him.

CHRISTINE

Hi there, are you looking for a good time?

LEWIS

What?

CHRISTINE (COYLY.)

I said do you want a good time? I can give you a good time. If you want a good time, come with me. If not, just say so.

Lewis looks her up and down.

LEWIS

I don't know.

LEANDRA

Tell him one hundred bucks, at your place.

CHRISTINE

One hundred dollars for a night at my place.

LEANDRA

Stand closer.

Christine moves closer.

LEWIS

Maybe, OK, sure.

They go into the house. Thelma is in the kitchen. Christine comes in with Lewis. Leandra follows.

CHRISTINE

Mom, this is, what's your name?

LEWIS

Lewis. Just Lewis.

THELMA

Hello, Lewis.

Lewis and Christine thread their way through the bags of trash to Christine's room. Leandra follows.

LEANDRA

I'll show you everything you need to do. Take your clothes off, slowly.

CHRISTINE

It's OK, I already know how.

> Lights fade out on the bedroom. Lights fade up on Thelma at the kitchen table.

> Christine comes into the kitchen and shows Thelma the hundred dollars. Thelma looks deeply into her daughter's eyes.

THELMA

Give me fifty of that, we need groceries.

> Christine gives Thelma half the money. Thelma crumples it in her hand and turns away.

THELMA

Are you going to get a real job?

CHRISTINE

That was a real job and that's a real hundred dollars.

> Leandra appears from the bedroom. Christine goes back to her.

LEANDRA

See how easy life can be, when you know how things are.

> Lights fade out. Lights fade up on the bedroom.

> Christine and Lewis are in bed. Lewis looks at Christine appreciatively.

LEWIS

So what's new with you? Still being stalked by the president?

CHRISTINE

How? Yeah, you know it. Ever since I've known you.

LEWIS

What do you mean? Ever since you've known me?

CHRISTINE

Every since I knew you I started imagining that I've been fucking the president.

LEWIS

I didn't know you were imagining that. Tell me about it.

CHRISTINE

I imagine that you're the president. Simple. That's it. I told you this before,

He leaned back smiling even more broadly.

LEWIS

I know but I like to see you sitting there naked telling me about it. Do you think Mr. President is good in bed? Is it because he's powerful? Like me?

CHRISTINE

At least as powerful as you Lewis. Hey listen, I have a question now.

LEWIS

What?

CHRISTINE

What do you do for a living Lewis? I'm surprised you haven't told me.

LEWIS

I'm a pipefitter. I work over in Hebron.

CHRISTINE

A pipefitter, what does that mean?

> Lewis sits up, clears his throat, and speaks as though reading from a book.

LEWIS

Pipefitters lay, install, assemble, fabricate, maintain, repair and troubleshoot mechanical piping systems carrying fuel, chemicals, water, steam and air in heating, cooling, lubricating and various other process piping systems.

CHRISTINE

You went to school for that?

LEWIS

You bet.

CHRISTINE

I never went to school. Well, I did really. My mother sent me to school. But I had outgrown all my clothes, and they were covered in a smell. No one would play with me; so I started going to places in my mind; places that were quiet and soft and bright. I was never really there. I guess the teachers thought there was something wrong with me. They sent me to a hospital and said I had something even my mother couldn't pronounce.

LEWIS

Oh.

CHRISTINE

No, but the good Lord gave me all that I need to do my job.

LEWIS (GRINS)

I can see that.

She sits and tucks her legs beneath her.

CHRISTINE
Good. I'm glad you can see that. You know I really should get dressed now.

LEWIS
Why? You should go out like this, you look fine just the way you are.

CHRISTINE
Very funny.

Projections of Mt. Everest appear out the window.

Leandra enters from the bathroom and crosses to the window.

The walls to the room swing open revealing projections, on the walls and out the window of the slopes of the mountain covered with dead bodies.

Christine looks out at Leandra.

CHRISTINE
I'm not here now, you know, I'm on Everest.

LEWIS
Everest? You mean the big mountain?

CHRISTINE
Yes. Everest is there right now, Everest is there and we are too, everyplace is there and here too. We're everyplace,

Christine turns back.

CHRISTINE
I tell you what, you can stay and it'll be on the house.

LEWIS (SMILING)

No, I really need to get home,

> Christine crosses her arms on her chest and closes her eyes.

CHRISTINE

Please, please, you need to stay. Please just one time. This time.

LEWIS

What's all this about Mount Everest.

> Christine gets back in the bed. Leandra comes back from the window and joins her.

LEWIS

No really, who were you talking to in the mirror?

CHRISTINE

Nobody. Look now, there, right now, right there, the tip of Mount Everest, windblown and icy. The wind is blowing, the wind is always blowing. Can you feel it? That's where we are right now, atop the peak of Mount Everest. This room is up high, too high to leave, can you feel the air? The air is thin. If you go out the door you will die. You die. Go on, try, just go on. Go on and try, you'll die from the frozen wind and the thin air, your body tumbling thousands of feet below, and smashing, landing, where? Who knows how far you'll fall, and where?

> Lewis listens and begins to worry.

CHRISTINE

Have you ever heard of George Mallory?

LEWIS

No.

CHRISTINE

He fell off Everest in 1921 and his body wasn't found until 1999. Isn't that amazing? I saw it in the newspaper in the hospital. I always read the newspapers in the hospital. There isn't much else to do in the hospital. You know.

LEWIS

What were you in the hospital for?

CHRISTINE

It really, well, it kind of was a hospital I suppose, it was a mental institution, a nut house, I was in the nut house for twenty years. I read about George Mallory who lay there on Mount Everest dead for seventy eight years with all the wind and cold and snow and ice whipping all around his body. You know?

LEWIS

OK.

CHRISTINE

I thought I was a lot like him you know, just lying there as good as dead in the nut house, the only difference being that in there there's heating in the winter and it doesn't snow, rain, and freeze on you; and it's hot in the summer though I bet it was hot in the summer on George Mallory where he lay there flat on his face all those years unmoving. Isn't it amazing how something can lie in the same place, not moving, for longer than we've been alive?

LEWIS

Sure, I guess so.

CHRISTINE

I saw an actual picture of him where they found him and all, he was on his stomach and his head was buried in the loose stones, his back and arm were bare and his buttocks were sticking out, his clothes had rotted off him, and there were holes in his buttocks, big holes in his ass cheeks, you could see they were black as night.

LEWIS

Why were you in the nut house, Christine?

CHRISTINE

I was crazy.

LEWIS

Crazy?

CHRISTINE

Yes. I just wasn't myself, I wasn't myself, I suppose, so yes, I was crazy.

LEWIS

But crazy means so many different things, we're all crazy at times, like how I was crazy that night when I forgot to call Allie and then I feel terrible about it in my head? Where was my head? I always called Allie before, I don't know,

CHRISTINE

Don't know what? What don't you know?

LEWIS

OK, I'll say it right out--there's something about you, Christine that makes me forget things. Nothing bad, you understand, please don't think that. But there's something.

CHRISTINE

Something? Like what?

LEWIS

Like how you went on and on about Mount Everest and this guy
Mallory,

CHRISTINE

Oh, yes, Mallory. Poor Mallory. He was just climbing along and
then, POW, down he goes, I wonder what it's like to fall that far?
And then to just lay there for seventy eight years. Actually it was
longer because the people that found him didn't bring him down,
they did an Anglican service over him and then piled stones on
top of him and left him there, it's they call a cairn burial.

LEWIS

Cairn burial?

CHRISTINE

Yes. Cairn burial. I read in a book that a cairn burial is just a
pile of stones, so my question is what keeps them from falling
all apart if they don't cement the stones in and they just stack
them on top of each other, Mallory might be laying right there
right now the way he did for seventy-eight years all uncovered.
And what if the cairn breaks down and the stones all scatter, so
that he'll be lying there for another seventy-eight years. What
do you think of that? Huh?

LEWIS

Well, I think that's enough talk of old mummified corpses lying
on mountains, do you think you could drive me back now?

Christine looks at Lewis insistently.

CHRISTINE

No, we can't get down from here, we're atop Mount Everest, you
need to stay the night before we can get down. It's too cold out-

side, the wind will die in fifteen minutes, but the cold won't. How about you stay the night?

CENTER LEWIS

Does that increase the price?

CHRISTINE

Why? Are you assuming that we will do something more tonight?

LEWIS

Yes, I guess I am assuming that.

CHRISTINE

Fifty dollars. Do you have that much?

LEWIS

You know I do.

> He hands over two hundred dollars

CHRISTINE

Two hundred? I'll go tell my mom you're staying the night.

> Lights fade up on Thelma, in the kitchen, watching the TV which flickers across her face.

> Thelma sits in her gray robe as Christine struggles down the stairs and across the living room kicking garbage bags aside that had fallen from the piles on each side blocking the pathway through, and she goes into the kitchen.

CHRISTINE

Mom, Lewis is staying the night, please stay out of my room while he's here.

THELMA

You know I don't like that. You know it's wrong to let them stay the night.

CHRISTINE

Puts money in our pockets, Mom. We need the money.

> Thelma looks up with raised eyebrows and grim mouth set. Leandra comes down to the kitchen and motions for Christine to go back.

CHRISTINE

Good night Mom. I'm going upstairs.

THELMA

OK. Night night, my dear. You are taking care of yourself, right?

> Christine leaves Thelma staring at her television and winds her way back through the trash with Leandra following.

LEANDRA

You're doing the right thing, it's deadly out there. Whoever leaves dies.

CHRISTINE

I just hope that mother or Lewis don't look out the window to see where they really are, they wouldn't be able to understand it, I don't know what they would do.

LEANDRA

Never mind that. It's too dark for them to see. Right now, you need to go take care of Lewis. He paid you the extra money. Besides, you like him. You even said that having sex with him is like having sex with the president.

CHRISTINE

It is.

> Christine and Leandra go back into the bedroom. Christine goes to the bed and Leandra sits on the chair at the Vanity.

> Christine wraps her arms around Lewis.

>> Lights fade out on the bed. Light fades up on Leandra, watching from the vanity. She smiles appreciatively. Light fades down on Leandra as light fades up downstage on Lewis, putting on his clothes.

LEWIS

I don't know if I'm going to go to Christine's any more. Christine is nice enough mostly but that house she lives in looks like it's sagging in on itself and will fall in any minute. I can't hardly make it to her room, it's all dark and I stumble over all the loose trash up along the stairs, but once I'm in, watch out! It's beautiful. Just like her. She's worth every dollar, every damned dollar. But she's a crazy goose too; crazy, crazy goose. Like going off on Mount Everest, that's spooky. Then she starts talking like there's somebody else there. It's like I'm not there anymore. It's just that she is so damned good at what she does.

I take back what I said about not knowing if I'll go back to be with her. Of course I'll go back to Christine. Yes you bet I will! She's got what it takes. She is so damned good. But now, when I get home to Allie, my wife. I want to be extra nice to her after what I've done. I'll take her dancing and I'll hold her close and try not to imagine that she's Christine. Besides, there's no harm done, in that a body is a body in the dark with your eyes closed after all. I can just keep everything that happened to me with Christine inside and Allie will never know about it. She'll just enjoy the dance, no matter what;

hot bodies pressed together like that is all, and one body is just as good as another body, isn't it? For sex, I mean. Just for sex.

> Light fades out. Lights fade up downstage where an area of trash opens up on the Deshler Borough Hall. There is a desk with a computer screen and keyboard.

> Mrs. Petersen, a watery-eyed woman, with thick glasses, sits behind the desk. Christine stands, with Leandra, in front of the desk. They are dressed identically in skirt, blouse, and sweater. Each has a matching silver studded purse. Christine refers to a piece of paper in her hand.

CHRISTINE

I'd like to see Mr. Barber.

MRS. PETERSEN

I'm sorry but Mister Barber is not here. He went down to Jefferson County today to handle a few things. What is the problem? I see that you have one of our notices there, is that what this is all about? How can I help you?

CHRISTINE

My mother got this notice on her door that says that she has two weeks to clean out her house and her yard before this Mister Barber is going to come down and do an inspection. I want to put in for an extension on that inspection. We need more than two weeks time to clean her place up. Also I understand there have been complaints?

> Mrs. Petersen makes an entry into the computer.

MRS. PETERSEN

Yes, there have been a total of thirty six complaints. Your name is Zidar, right?

CHRISTINE

Yes, yes, but who did the complaining?

MRS. PETERSEN

I can't tell you that Miss. That will come out in court if this comes to that.

CHRISTINE

In court?

MRS. PETERSEN

Yes, in court. If we decide to evict you and you appeal, you'll have to do so at the county court house in Hebron.

CHRISTINE

If you decide to evict us? What do you mean, evict us? My mom owns that house. How can you evict us?

MRS. PETERSEN

You've gotten health code violations and thirty six complaints. Listen, the best thing for you to do is to simply clean your place up and pass the inspection, and your troubles here will be over.

> Christine glances at Leandra who whispers into her ear. Christine looks directly into Mrs. Petersen's eyes.

CHRISTINE

I want to talk to Mister Barber's boss.

MRS. PETERSEN (SMILES POINTEDLY.)

You are talking to her.

CHRISTINE (TAKEN ABACK)

And please, what is your name?

MRS. PETERSEN

Petersen. I'm Mrs. Petersen.

> Christine turns back to Leandra who whispers to her
> again. She takes a pen out of her purse and jots down the
> name on the notice. Leandra whispers again.

CHRISTINE

Listen, Miss Petersen let's be real, what will it take to make this
go away?

MRS. PETERSEN

Make what go away?

CHRISTINE

This notice. What will it take to make it go away?

MRS. PETERSEN

You need to clean your place up,

CHRISTINE

No I mean how much will it take? How many dollars?

> Christine and Leandra place their hands on their silver
> studded bags. Miss Petersen's eyebrows raise. She taps
> her pencil on the desk.

MRS. PETERSEN

Now don't you try to bribe me, bribing me is against the law.

CHRISTINE (CONFIDENTIALLY.)

Enough dollars will make anything go away. Let's say, three hundred dollars? How about I pay three hundred dollars and you wipe
all this off the records?

MRS. PETERSEN

I can't wipe it off the records. Everything's all registered in the system. Your inspection date is what it says on that notice. Have the place cleaned up and be ready. And don't try to bribe me again or I'll call for a sheriff. Spend the three hundred on a cleanup service. If you're so anxious to use money to make this go away, that is the way to do it. Are we clear?

Christine glances at Leandra; Leandra whispers to her.

CHRISTINE

I want a list of the people who have complained.

MRS. PETERSEN

I can't give you that. I told you already.

CHRISTINE

Then I want to speak to your boss.

MRS. PETERSEN

My boss is the Mayor, and he isn't in. Go to his office though, there'll be a receptionist there and you can make an appointment to see him.

CHRISTINE

OK, I will do that, but off the record, I mean can I talk off the record without you calling for an officer, as you say?

MRS. PETERSEN

Depends, but go on.

CHRISTINE

I will give you five hundred dollars in your hand right here, right now to make this thing go away. You see, my Mom is very feeble.

A lot of that stuff has value to her. She has to have the time to go through everything. I'll tell you what, push the deadline back by a month, and I'll give you the two hundred dollars, just to push the deadline back or you can have the five hundred to make the whole thing go away. You'd be doing a good deed. Plus you'd have a pocketful of money. It's just between me and you. What do you say?

MRS. PETERSEN

Go talk to the Mayor. And please, none of this bribery talk with him. He'll have you locked up. He's a straight arrow. I'm warning you, miss. Don't you dare.

> Christine clutches the notice. She and Leandra cross to the other side of the stage.
>
> Lights cross fade from the desk to a spot on
>
> Christine and Leandra conspire. Christine listens intently.

LEANDRA

You have to change your approach. You have to tell him that this notice from the city is a mistake that needs to be corrected. You have to tell him that the place is spotless now. You have to tell him that the order was written for somebody else, and not for you. He might ask, "How did your name get on it?" You tell him that it was a mistake, just one of those crazy mistakes. The place is spotless. That is how you talk to a Mayor. Don't talk about bribe money. That Miss Petersen was too low level to know what's really going on. But I'll bet they lose records all the time at this place. And what's with the inspector's name? Mister Barber? An even lower flunky than the one you already talked to.

> Lights fade up on the desk

LEANDRA

There's the woman Mrs. Petersen was talking about. Go to it Christine.

Lights fade out on Christine and Leandra as they cross to the desk. An office area opens out of the trash.

Mary, a small woman sits at the desk writing fast in a yellow legal pad. She looks up from under the dome of her blonde hair and through her gold rimmed glasses.

MARY

Can I help you?

CHRISTINE

Yes, I need to make an appointment to see the mayor.

MARY (PUTTING DOWN HER PEN.)

Regarding?

CHRISTINE (HOLDING UP THE NOTICE.)

Regarding this, my mother got it by mistake and Mrs. Petersen downstairs said I need to see the Mayor to correct it.

MARY

But Mrs. Petersen and Mister Barber handle all these types of things. The Mayor would just tell you to see them.

Leandra whispers to Christine.

CHRISTINE (TIGHTENING)

That's the problem. They said that they won't help me. They said that I need to see the Mayor but he's not in today, so she told me that I have to make an appointment.

MARY

All right.

She makes an entry on the keyboard and refers to the computer screen. Leandra whispers into Christine's ear and nods toward the computer

CHRISTINE

Miss?

The woman looks up from the schedule.

MARY

Yes?

CHRISTINE

Is that computer hooked into the system where these notices are kept?

MARY

Yes, why?

Christine leans down and speaks softly.

CHRISTINE

You know, this notice was a mistake, it shouldn't have been sent out to us. The people downstairs say they can't delete it. They told me that the Mayor's office could delete it. That's why they sent me up here. To tell you to delete it.

MARY

They said it was OK to delete it?

CHRISTINE

Yes they said that.

Christine looks Mary straight in the eye.

MARY

But that's not true that they can't delete it. Why did they say they couldn't delete it?

CHRISTINE

They said, well they said they wouldn't delete it. There's a long story that I have to tell the mayor about my mother to explain it all, and they wouldn't listen. And so I said, well then let me talk to your boss, and Mrs. Petersen said her boss is the Mayor. So I'm here, sorry if I confused things, it's not that they can't delete it, they just won't is all. Anyway, when is the mayor free tomorrow?

MARY

He's free at three, or four. But I'm just going to warn you, if Petersen and Barber won't take it off the books, the Mayor won't either. I know how these things go.

> Christine leans down again, taking a stack of bills out of her purse.

CHRISTINE

I bet this would get you to delete the notice.

> She opens her hand before the woman. She holds three one hundred dollar bills.

MARY

What? You're bribing me?

CHRISTINE

I never said that.

MARY

Oh yes you are. Put that away and I will try to forget it.

CHRISTINE

But, it's three hundred dollars. Three hundred dollars is a lot of money for me.

MARY

I can see that, and if you don't put it back I'll be forced to call an officer. Here, let me see your notice, what kind of notice is it?

> Christine hands the notice over. Mary squints into the piece of paper.

MARY

This just says that your house will be inspected in two weeks. Why is it being inspected? Let's see, health hazard, it says. Why don't you just clean up the health hazard instead of coming down here to argue with us? The Mayor won't be able to help you. He won't override the code enforcement folks. What's the health hazard?

CHRISTINE

My mother has a little trash around the place, that's all.

MARY

A little trash? You mean like hoarding?

CHRISTINE

I, I wouldn't go as far as that, but she's an old woman, she doesn't understand all this. Can't we just leave her alone until she passes? Then I can clean the place out, right quick.

MARY

How old is she?

CHRISTINE

Sixty-three.

MARY

She's not that old. She might live the next thirty years. She should be able to handle this. Is she in good health?

Leandra turns to Christine and whispers.

LEANDRA

She's got a really bad case of asthma.

Christine turns to Mary.

CHRISTINE

She's got a really bad case of asthma.

MARY

Well, cleaning the place up will improve that.

CHRISTINE

No it won't, the case is chronic. Oh, you don't know how sick she is. This whole notice and inspection thing is killing her and making her asthma worse. I...

The Deputy Mayor, a tall man in a neat suit and tie and with slicked back hair enters. He speaks to Mary.

DEPUTY MAYOR

Mary, is this young lady here to see the mayor?

MARY

Yes, but the Mayor is out today.

The Deputy Mayor looks Christine over and smiles.

DEPUTY MAYOR

Can I help? I'm the deputy mayor. I handle things when the mayor is away. I happen to have a moment to spare. Here, let me see that notice.

Christine hands him the notice. He looks at it carefully.

DEPUTY MAYOR

Zidar? Are you related to Thelma Zidar?

CHRISTINE

Yes, yes, I'm her daughter.

He nods thoughtfully as Mary scowls.

DEPUTY MAYOR

You can just appeal this. Do you just want to have the inspection moved back? So you have more time to clean up? Is this a hoarding situation?

CHRISTINE (HESITANTLY)

Yes, it is.

DEPUTY MAYOR

Mary, give this woman a form to file for an extension,

MARY

But look at the notice, it says that this is the final notice, no extensions.

DEPUTY MAYOR (SMILING)

Around here, there's no such thing as a final notice. This woman's mother is sick. We've got to take that into consideration.

MARY

But that's already been taken into consideration. It says they've had the date moved back five times.

DEPUTY MAYOR

Never mind that, Mary; give her the form. This is America. We care about people here.

He turns and walks back toward his office. Mary gives Christine the form.

MARY

Fill out this form and take it back to Miss Petersen. But let me warn you, it will get you nowhere, I don't know why he's saying what he's saying, you've already gotten a final notice there.

Christine looks at the form.

CHRISTINE

Thank you.

Mary nods and scowls. Christine turns to leave as Leandra leans in to her. They whisper.

LEANDRA

I wonder what her problem is. It's like they want to throw you out of your own house.

CHRISTINE

I know. But the deputy mayor said it would work. Did you see his eyes?

LEANDRA

Yes.

CHRISTINE

We're in good hands with him, I can feel it. That Mary doesn't know what she's talking about, come on lets go.

Mary stares incredulously at Christine. Christine turns back to her and glares.

She holds up the form and rushes across the stage to the kitchen

Lights fade out on the city office. Lights fade up on Thelma sitting at the kitchen table amongst the trash as Christine rushes in through the door, holding up the form. Leandra follows her.

CHRISTINE

Our problems are solved. We just need to fill this out.

Thelma grabs the form, looks at it quickly, crumples it up and tosses it into the piles of garbage.

THELMA

That's nonsense, they just gave you this form to get rid of you. Our inspection notice said the notice is final; this one is for real.

CHRISTINE

No! The deputy mayor gave this to me, he was a nice man, he meant what he said, I just know it.

THELMA

He just wanted you out of there and to leave because you were probably being a pest, like you always are.

CHRISTINE

I am not a pest! I was just trying to help us! We went down there to help you!

Thelma snaps toward her, eyes on fire.

THELMA

We? We went down there? Bullshit! What are you talking about? We went down there? What do you mean we? Are you going crazy again and trying to give me one more thing to worry about?

Christine stands still, holding her breath in with Leandra standing behind her.

CHRISTINE

I was never crazy!

THELMA

Yes you were, you had that imaginary friend. Apparently you still have her.

CHRISTINE

I don't have imaginary friends, I have real friends!

THELMA

What real friends? No one comes to see you but those johns you bring in here.

CHRISTINE

They are my friends!

THELMA

That's crazy and you know it. Why can't you just stay in your room and leave things alone?

CHRISTINE

Crazy? How dare you call me crazy? Damn you, look at how you keep this damned house of yours! It's your fault we're getting kicked out.

THELMA

We're not getting kicked out.

CHRISTINE

Yes we are, because of all this! Where are we going to go, Mom?

    Christine swung her arm against a wall of stacked trash bags and the wall falls completely burying Thelma's chair and blocking their way. Thelma stands shaking, knee-deep in the avalanche of trash.

THELMA (SCREAMS)

Damn you Christine! I ought to throw you out of here. You're nothing but trouble. Look what you've done, you damned slut,

CHRISTINE

This Goddamned slut pays all the bills, Mom, the bills! Now clean up your shit, all your shit's blocking the way.

THELMA

You knocked it down, you need to help me.

CHRISTINE

I don't need to do anything to help you. This house full of trash is yours. I bring the money in. I don't enjoy what I do, but like every other God-damned thing I do, I do it for you, you crazy hoarder bitch!

THELMA

Martin wouldn't put up with talk like that, he's here all the time, his spirit is. If he was more than a spirit he would brain you for talking to me like that.

CHRISTINE

He's dead! Get it through your head, he's dead!

Stricken, Thelma clutched her breast theatrically and sinks into the pile of trash bags, while Christine and Leandra make their way past her and up toward Christine's room.

CHRISTINE

I hate her.

LEANDRA

You do now, but it will pass,

CHRISTINE

No it won't. I hate her, I hate her house and I hate her mess.

They rush up the stairs.

CHRISTINE (SCREAMS)

Five hundred dollars, Mother! I'm good for five hundred. I don't see you turning it down! Five hundred dollars!

Christine throws herself on the bed. Leandra lays down next to her and cradles her.

Sound of a knock at the door.

Christine suddenly jumps up and rushes through the trash to the front door. She opens it with difficulty, pushing against piles of plastic bags. Mr. Tanady, a dark haired, portly, middle-aged man, stands there smiling.

TANADY

Christine! Good to see you again.

CHRISTINE (DISAPPOINTED.)

Where is Mr. Tanady? Mr. Tanady's supposed to be here at seven. Who are you?

Tanady looks around and back.

TANADY

I'm Mr. Tanady, Ronald Tanady. We have an appointment at seven. I've been here before.

They stand nose to nose at the door.

CHRISTINE

Don't get me wrong, Sir, I'll still do you. I don't mind that Ronnie sent someone else in his place. As long as your money's good. But tell me, do you know why Ronnie sent you here in his place?

TANADY

I don't understand.

CHRISTINE (STUDYING HIS EYES)

Never mind.

> Christine leans out through the doorway, takes his hand in hers and pulls him in.

CHRISTINE

Come on in. If you got money, I don't care if you're not Ronnie. You do look just like him though. Your disguise is very nice. Are you going to keep the disguise on while we do it? Or are you going to let me see who you really are?

TANADY (STEPPING OVER TRASH.)

I... I'm not wearing a disguise.

CHRISTINE (WINKS)

OK. I'll go along with it. If this is how Ronnie wants it to be, I'm OK with it, too.

> They squeeze past the clutter and go up the stairs. Christine kicks the trash aside and opens the door. They go in. Tanady sits on the bed and pulls off his shoes. Christine looks at him carefully.

CHRISTINE

Come on, before we go any further. Take off the mask.

TANADY

I… Christine, I'm not wearing a mask, I'm Ronnie, look, look.

> He pulls his wallet out and hands his driver's license to her. She examines his credit cards very carefully and hands them back.

CHRISTINE

Well, I suppose if Ronald trusted you enough to carry his wallet and carry all his cards I suppose I can trust you too. I noticed money in there, you know you owe me three hundred for tonight, right? Did Ronald tell you?

> Tanady puts the cards into his wallet

TANADY

Yes, Christine, Mr. Tanady told me.

CHRISTINE (STUDYING HIM.)

I just wish I knew who you really are.

TANADY

I am Ronald Tanady. But who am I to complain. I've got the money, love, so let's get into bed.

> Leandra enters from the bathroom and gets into the bed with them.

> Lights fade out.

> The voices of Christine, Mr. Tanady, and Leandra moan in ecstasy.

TANADY (IN THE DARK)

Oh Christine! You are continually amazing!

> Lights fade up on the bedroom.

CHRISTINE

What do you mean "continually"? Isn't this our first time?

TANADY

Oh, yeah, right, I'm not Mr. Tanady. I'm wearing a mask. Jeez Christine, believe what you want to.

CHRISTINE (To LEANDRA.)

That mask stayed on perfectly?

LEANDRA

Ask him, go on and ask him.

CHRISTINE

Will I be seeing the real Mr. Tanady again? Or will he be sending you from now on?

TANADY

I… I don't know.

CHRISTINE

I have a test for you, this will prove that you're not really Mr. Tanady. Ready?

TANADY

Sure, fine.

CHRISTINE

What are you most guilty about?

TANADY

What?

Leandra squeezes Christine's hand under the sheet.

CHRISTINE

I said, what did Mr. Tanady do as a child that he's most guilty about?

He looks at her and immediately props himself up on his elbows.

TANADY

Christine, you know the answer to that question as well as I do. Do you mean to say, that if I was an imposter, you'd repeat what I told you in confidence?

CHRISTINE

I didn't say I'd repeat it, I'm not going to tell you what I know, that would ruin the test, I just said tell me what it was.

He looks down and takes the sheet between his fingers. He looks her in the eye.

TANADY

I don't want to talk about that, I'm not in the mood. I should never have told you that to begin with.

CHRISTINE

You mean about what you did in school.

TANADY

Right.

CHRISTINE

Then you don't know. See? You're not Mr. Tanady.

TANADY

Christine, I don't understand this crazy talk, what's the matter with you?

CHRISTINE

Crazy? Are you saying that I'm crazy?

TANADY

No, I didn't call you crazy, I just said this is enough of this kind of talk.

CHRISTINE

What kind of talk? Crazy talk?

TANADY

OK, fine, yes! Enough of this crazy talk!

CHRISTINE

If you think I talk crazy, then you must think I am crazy. See you just proved you're not him. Mr. Tanady is a true gentleman, he'd never call me crazy. He respects me. Plus you didn't know what he's ashamed of. That's two strikes against you.

Tanady touches Christine.

TANADY

How about some more now, Christine? Your crazy talk is getting me all worked up.

CHRISTINE

OK, OK, sure. Come on.

She put her arms around him. Leandra snuggles in and embraces Mr. Tanady.

CHRISTINE

Hey, hey Mr. Fake Tanady. I got you. You still don't know what Tanady told me he was guilty about. You know what?

TANADY

What?

CHRISTINE

You're not Tanady. The balls of you, pretending to be someone that I cared for! Get out of my house, pay me the money that you owe me, and then get the fuck out of here!

TANADY

But I am Ronald. I am Mr. Tanady, You're crazy! You are, you really are, here, take your damn money!

> He stands by the bed and grabs at his clothes balled up on the chair. He pulls money from the pocket of his pants and throws it on her bed. Christine snatches it up, counting it quickly.

CHRISTINE

You are not Mr. Tanady because you don't know what he told me he was most guilty about! Well, don't ever come to see me again, and tell Mr. Tanady, I don't want to see him again either.

> Ronald pulls on his pants. She sits half up.

CHRISTINE

You look afraid. Why are you afraid?

TANADY

I'm not afraid. I'm not scared, Christine.

CHRISTINE

You know what I would be scared of?

TANADY

No, what?

> Sound of wind. Walls swing open. Fade up Projection of dead bodies on the slopes of Mt. Everest.

CHRISTINE

To be on Mount Everest with all the dead bodies that are laying all around.

TANADY

What dead bodies? Where?

Tanady slips on his jacket.

CHRISTINE

Mount Everest. There are over two hundred dead bodies on Mount Everest, people that fell climbing or passed out or just froze to death. They're still there, they're just sitting there, laying there, when you climb up you pass them. They never change. They just lay there. No years pass by them. They are like rocks and stones. Imagine a place like that? What an awful place that would be, lying there, your eyes burned out, just blank holes staring up at the skies, forever.

TANADY

I have to go Christine.

CHRISTINE

Oh. All right. Tell Ronald that I said hello and that he better get his fat butt in here next week.

TANADY

I will. Take care of yourself Christine.

CHRISTINE

You still look afraid. Are you?

TANADY

I'm not afraid.

CHRISTINE

Want me to show you out?

TANADY

No need. Goodbye Christine.

CHRISTINE

Bye.

Tanady leaves. Christine rolls over toward Leandra.

Lights fade out. Light fades up on Tanady.

TANADY

What is this nonsense about me being somebody else? I know she spent a lot of years in the big crazy house. But I thought they let her out of there when she was better. I thought they kept people in when they have big problems. Christine seems to have big problems.

What I told Christine was that when I was at the start of sixth grade I chose to be feared. I had a big growth spurt, I was twice the size of other kids. They thought I was a giant freak. I used to spend all recess just sitting alone on the blacktop at the corner of the playground, pounding it with stones and breaking off pieces from the corner where the dirt began. Every recess, far away from everybody, breaking up the blacktop. So I targeted kids I knew were thinking I was a freak; there was one named Mark. He was playing baseball. I tripped him running the bases. He sprawled face-first into the dirt. I pulled him up by the hair; his friends just stared at me. Mark tried to stand up to me but I punched him hard in the stomach. He doubled over and I pushed him down in the dirt. I got a bat and started swinging it. "I'm in the game now, I'm up. Throw already, or you'll get what Mark got. Maybe even worse." The pitcher threw some balls. I swung and missed. He struck me out with three pitches. Then the damned catcher said,

"You're out." I spun around and grabbed him by the hair. I shook him like a rag doll and threw him down. I swung the bat and he stayed down. I was the big man. Mark stopped playing the games at recess and stayed to himself and took my place at the asphalt corner. Everybody was afraid of me, and it felt good.

All I ever wanted was to feel good. All I ever wanted was to be with nice people. This is why I thank God for Christine. She delivers me from myself. She accepts me as myself. But sometimes I don't know about her. Like tonight when she thought I was somebody else. It might be good to be somebody else. Somebody who hadn't done what I'd done. Someone who wasn't a monster, because once a monster, always a monster. Those kids will never forget me. And as long as they remember me that way, that is the way that I am, no matter what I do to change, no matter the number of times that Christine holds me. They are always there on that playground, terror in their eyes. It will never be over. I was a monster, always will be.

> Light fades out on Tanady. Flickering TV light fades
> up on Thelma's face. Lights fade up on the kitchen.

Thelma sits in the kitchen in her bathrobe. Christine comes down from her room, removes a bag of trash from another chair and eases into it.

CHRISTINE
Did you fill out that appeals form, Mom?

THELMA
What appeals form?

CHRISTINE
The one I got at borough hall the other day, remember? I went down there to ask about changing our deadline to get the place cleaned up?

THELMA

Oh, that form. No I haven't filled it out yet.

Christine pulls a pen from her pocket.

CHRISTINE

Where is the form, I'll fill it out. I want to get it back to them today. Please Mom, this is important.

THELMA

I don't know where it is. In here somewhere, I suppose.

CHRISTINE

Stop looking at that TV and look at me! We need to find that form now! They promised me an extension. They're talking about eviction, Mom. Where's your head?

Thelma turns and points at Christine.

THELMA

How dare you talk to me like that.

CHRISTINE

Never mind how I talk to you, find that form, now!

Heavily Thelma rises from her chair, turns and half heartedly starts to pick through the trash.

THELMA

If your Father were alive you wouldn't be talking to me like that Christine. He'd never stand for it.

Christine reaches up and switches off the TV,

CHRISTINE

Sure, there are a lot of things here he wouldn't be standing for if he was alive.

Thelma scowls and pokes through the trash.

THELMA
What is that supposed to mean?

CHRISTINE
It means that this house wouldn't be in this shape. This wouldn't be happening! I cannot believe you lost that form!

Thelma adamantly turns on Christine.

THELMA
I didn't lose it! I just can't find it right now. What other things? What are you trying to say to me, Christine? Why don't you right out and say it?

CHRISTINE
I don't have to say anything right out, Mom. Find that form, if you don't find it I'll have to go down and get another one, damn it anyway!

Christine gets up and kicks her way through the trash, and heads for her room.

THELMA (YELLS.)
Where are you going?

CHRISTINE
Let me know when you find it.

THELMA
I...

CHRISTINE
Just find it!

Christine squeezes past the stacks of trash and goes up the stairs

Lights fade up in Christine's room

Christine enters her room and sinks into her chair

CHRISTINE

Leandra, Leandra where are you?

Christine stands and looks into the mirror.

Martin's Projection appears on the back wall by the bathroom door (or live Martin enters from the bathroom.)

MARTIN'S PROJECTION

There's no point in going after your mother, honey. What is done is done. There's no going back. There is just forward. Now go down and take care of that damned stinking Deshler borough hall. I'll show you how it ought to have been done.

Christine goes down to the kitchen, knocking over a bag of trash in the process. She crosses go to Thelma, who still hunches over the table, searching for the appeals form.

MARTIN'S PROJECTION

Get your mother ready, we're taking her to borough hall.

CHRISTINE

Mom, get your socks and shoes on, we're going to borough hall.

Thelma stops poking at the trash, looks up and sees Martin's projection. She stares in shock, quickly gets up, turns away and starts poking through a bag of trash by the door.

THELMA

Go somewhere? I can't go somewhere. I never go anywhere, you know that.

Christine pulls her back to the table, sits her in her chair. She raises up a foot, puts the socks and shoes that were there under the kitchen table on her.

Martin's Projection smiles.

MARTIN'S PROJECTION
We're going down to borough hall to fix things.

CHRISTINE
We're going to fix things the way they ought to be fixed. The way Daddy would have fixed our problems.

THELMA
Our problems?

MARTIN'S PROJECTION
I am here to show you what it means to solve a problem.

THELMA
But you're...

MARTIN'S PROJECTION
Dead? Who me? No. I was, so therefore I still am. Now I am here to show you I was never dead.

Thelma stands up next to Christine and takes her hand. They go out the door.

THELMA
We are going to lock the house, right?

MARTIN'S PROJECTION
No, it'd be a blessing if someone were to come in while we were gone and take out all the shit that you've got in here.

THELMA

I haven't found the form yet Christine, I know you wanted me to find the form but I couldn't find it,

MARTIN'S PROJECTION

We won't need any damned form.

> Lights fade out. Borough Hall office folds out of the trash. Lights fade up on the Borough Hall office desk.

> Barber, a low cut man in a loose suit and a brushed back, mussed hair, sits at the desk. Martin, dressed as he was in the projection, enters with Christine and Thelma.

MARTIN

It would have been done in negative thirty years if I'd been here, see, the problem is I haven't been here yet. But I'm here now. And it counts.

CHRISTINE

Can she come in here in that bathrobe?

MARTIN

Sure she can.

> Martin takes Thelma by the arm and eases her over to the desk. Barber, looks up,

BARBER

Can I help you folks?

MARTIN

Easy there. Are you the one trying to put this pitiful old woman out of her house and onto the street?

Barber pushes back his hair and sharply thrusts out his nose. Christine flinches. Thelma looks down to the floor.

BARBER

Who's trying to do that? Who's trying to put that old lady out on the street? Fill me in here. What're you talking about? I can't help you if I don't know what you're talking about.

Martin grips his wife's arm tighter.

MARTIN

Next week they're coming to inspect her house, and then they're going to put her out,

BARBER (SUDDENLY REALIZING.)

Oh, this is the hoarder case on Pickwick. You're the Zidar's. Oh, I know. Yes, there have been multiple complaints received and multiple warnings given.

MARTIN

What's your name son?

BARBER

My name? Why do you want my name?

MARTIN

Because I'll need it when I speak to your boss.

BARBER

What are you going to speak to my boss about?

MARTIN

Because you're calling this poor woman names. Hoarder, you say, well she's no hoarder! Just needs a little slack cut to give her time to tidy the place up. You...

BARBER (REFUSING TO BE BULLIED)

Sir, there's been an order issued and a notice given. They're going out to inspect, she's had multiple warnings. I suggest you take your energy back home and use it to clean up the place. The whole street is up in arms! And, may I remind you, they're all taxpayers,

MARTIN

No, you wait a minute, son...

BARBER

I'm not your son, and no, you let me finish; the taxpayers on the block are concerned and our job here is to address whatever it is when the taxpayers get concerned.

MARTIN

This woman here is a taxpayer too. Listen, we're wasting enough time here already. You're just a flunkie. Get me your boss.

BARBER

Fine!

Barber shuffles off.

MARTIN

Now we're getting somewhere. Bosses get to be where they are by having a brain, not like this flunkie. Listen, Christine, I need you to pipe up too. Pipe up and speak up for your mother.

CHRISTINE (LOOKING INTO HIS EYES.)

I think you're doing just fine.

MARTIN

This is for you, Christine; you've got to speak up for your mother! Speak up!

THELMA

I don't do this! I don't go out for these things!

Thelma hurries back to the kitchen.

Lights fade out on the city office. The flickering from the TV reflects on Thelma's face.

Goes straight for the kitchen table, pulls off her shoes and socks while clutching a piece of yellow paper.

Lights fade up on the kitchen

Christine enters and points to the paper.

CHRISTINE

Is that the form? There in your hand?

Thelma looks at the form. She turns back toward the kitchen.

THELMA

No, I can't find it. This is the notice that they gave me saying they were going to inspect. I can't find the appeals form. I'm sorry.

Christine switches the TV off. Martin looks around impatiently.

MARTIN (LOUDLY.)

What's taking so long? What is the damned problem? They're so worried about those other damned taxpayers, but what about us? What about us, why aren't they worried about us? Hurry up! We don't have all day!

The flickering on Thelma's face stops.

CHRISTINE

OK Mom, we're going down to borough hall to get a new form and you are coming with me.

THELMA

Why should I come with you? You went by yourself before.

CHRISTINE

Come on, get up. Here are your shoes and socks. We're going together.

> Lights fade up on the office as Christine helps
> Thelma with her shoes and socks.

> Mrs. Peterson enters with Barber. She sits at the desk
> with Barber behind her. Martin stands in front of her.

MRS. PETERSON

I hear you've got a complaint about Mister Barber here. What is it? He says that you're the ones being rude and annoying, so before you even say anything, don't you dare be rude or I will have security show you the door. Is that understood?

MARTIN

Rude? Rude, us? No, but I could say the same thing about Mister Barberpole here, is that what your little flunkie said? We're rude?

MRS. PETERSON

His name is Mr. Barber, and he's not a flunkie he's a...

MARTIN

Never mind him! He's not important. Here's what's important, we are trying help a poor old woman with a little more time to tidy up her place before you inspect it, how about a couple of months? Give her a month, or two.

MRS. PETERSON

Don't you use that tone with me!

Christine and Thelma pushed past the chair and TV and trash bags, and head out the door.

THELMA

Aren't you going to lock the house?

CHRISTINE

No, it'd be a blessing if someone were to come in while we were gone and take out all the stuff that you've got in there. You've got too much stuff in there.

MRS. PETERSON

And no, there won't be any extensions. There have been nine warnings issued over a two-year period. The tenth warning is the final warning. There can be no appeal on a final warning. The city inspector will be there next week and the place better be clean.

Barber stands smiling behind Mrs. Peterson Christine and Thelma enter the office

MARTIN

I want to see your boss!

MRS. PETERSON

My boss is the Mayor, he's upstairs. But you need an appointment. Go up and see his secretary and see if she will give you one!

MARTIN

You and your boy here will be in for a load of trouble.

MRS. PETERSON

I don't think so.

MARTIN

We'll see.

Mrs. Peterson and Barber exit as Martin turns to Christine and Thelma.

MARTIN

Big deal, big deal Mayor, well he's just a man, like me.

CHRISTINE

Mom, we're going to make a big stink today! We're going to make a big stink and that's why I wanted you to come along. I want them to see the sweet little person that they want to throw out into the street.

THELMA

Sweet little person? What a nice thing to say.

CHRISTINE

Well, it's true Mom.

Mary, with gold rimmed glasses, sits at the desk. She looks up under her bubble of blonde hair.

MARTIN (ROUGHLY)

We need to see the Mayor now. The people at the code enforcement window said we needed to see the Mayor today.

MARY

The Mayor is not seeing anyone today. I can make you an appointment for next week,

MARTIN

No! We need to see him today. There's no time, we...

THE Deputy Mayor comes in behind them. They turn in unison.

DEPUTY MAYOR

Can I help you?

MARTIN

Who are you; another second rate flunkie I suppose?

DEPUTY MAYOR

I am the deputy Mayor and you seem to be in need of some help.

MARTIN

The town is going to put an old woman in the street and we're here to put a stop to it.

DEPUTY MAYOR

Really? It should be just a simple matter filling out an appeals form, we have them right here in this file.

MARTIN

No! You, you buzz the Mayor and tell him we need to see him right now!

Martin, Christine and Thelma turn back to Mary.

MARY

I'm sorry you'll have to make an appointment.

MARTIN

I said right now!

DEPUTY MAYOR

Sir, just calm down. Do as she says, use the appeals form.

Martin pushes the Deputy Mayor away.

MARTIN

No! Now!

The mayor barges in.

MAYOR

What is this? Who are you?

MARTIN

You're the one I'm looking for. You!

> Martin points and advances on the Mayor.

MAYOR

I warn you, keep back.

MARTIN

You! I demand…!

> Martin advances on the Mayor. In one smooth sweeping motion the Mayor pulls a forty-five from inside his suit coat, raises, cocks it and fires a bullet into Martin's heart. Martin falls. Christine and Thelma stop suddenly and return to the house as

> > Lights fade out. Flickering TV fades up on Thelma's face. Kitchen lights fade up.

> Christine helps Thelma takes off her socks at the kitchen table.

CHRISTINE

Did you hear that?

THELMA

No.

CHRISTINE

Are you sure?

THELMA

Sure. I didn't hear nothing.

CHRISTINE

We can't keep doing this, Mom? We've got to deal with all of this. Did you find that form yet?

THELMA

Not yet, but it's around here somewhere.

     Lights fade out. Lights fade up on Christine's room

  Francis Serdon, a bulky man with an intense smile lies in bed. Christine and Leandra enter from the bathroom and get into the bed, surrounding Serdon.

CHRISTINE

Francis, where were you Monday?

SERDON

I was at work.

CHRISTINE

All day?

SERDON

Yep,

CHRISTINE

You weren't at work, I saw you following me all day. I saw you at the Seven-Eleven Monday morning. You were watching me buy the papers.

SERDON

What?

CHRISTINE

You were at the Seven-Eleven pretending to be one of those Spanish guys who works behind the counter.

He looks at her.

                    SERDON
Oh, I get it. You're off again.

    He falls back on the pillow

                    CHRISTINE
You put on a disguise. How did you get it to look so real? You even
looked smaller, how do you make yourself look smaller like that?

                    SERDON
I got the costume from Party City.

        She glances over at Leandra who smiles and nods at her to
        go on. She turns back to Serdon.

                    CHRISTINE
Party City? They sell plastic bag costumes. This was a disguise.
If you're going to watch me, why not just be yourself? I wouldn't
mind running into you outside of this room, I'd say hi and we
could even have a nice conversation. I wouldn't pretend to not
know you. But in disguise, I wouldn't dare talk to you any more
after you said what you said to me in that disguise. Why couldn't
you just talk to me regular even if you felt you had to hide seeing
me and be disguised?

                    SERDON
What did the Seven-Eleven guy say?

                    CHRISTINE
No! See there, it wasn't some guy, it was you!

                    SERDON
What did I say?

CHRISTINE

You know. You were there.

> He rolls over and gently fondles Christine's breasts. She pushes his hand down

SERDON

OK, enough about that, how about some more honey?

CHRISTINE

No! Don't try and distract me,

SERDON

But sweetheart, this is why I pay you.

> She pushed his hand completely off her.

CHRISTINE

First I need to know why you are doing what you are doing. It wasn't just at the Seven-Eleven, you were at my doctor's. I said, oh come off it Francis, be real. You pretended to be confused and just told me to lie down and you examined me, like a doctor. Why did you need to pretend to be a doctor?

> He lays the back of his hand on his forehead.

SERDON

Christine, I don't like it when you are like this. Snap out of it,

> She raises herself on her elbow and points at him.

CHRISTINE

Snap out of what? I want to know why you're following me around and watching where I go when I leave my house.

SERDON

I don't know what you are talking about. If you are playing with me, stop it. This is a real turn off, Christine. Stop the fooling around.

CHRISTINE

Fooling around? You think I'm the one fooling around? You're
the one that's doing the fooling around here. Come on, tell me,
how you get the real people to let you take their place?

SERDON

What do you mean? To get the real people to do what?

CHRISTINE

Like the doctor or the Seven-Eleven guy. This has to be a big
conspiracy. Do you remember what you did at the grocery store
on Wednesday?

SERDON

Sure, Christine. I remember, you want to hear that I remember,
then I remember.

CHRISTINE

How did you do it? You so nearly blew my mind,

SERDON

How did I blow your mind?

> Christine stares directly into his eyes.

CHRISTINE

When I was going up and down the aisles, the people in every aisle were all you in disguise. This is amazing, I remember
thinking to myself. How did you do that? Every one of you
looked perfect.

> The bedroom walls open out. Projections of a
> frumpy old housewife, a young Asian girl, an old
> man wobbling on his cane, a nun fade up on the
> walls and stare down at Christine.

CHRISTINE

You were a frumpy old housewife, a young Asian girl, an old man wobbling on his cane, a nun!

SERDON

A nun?

> Christine gets more agitated. She starts kneading her belly to sooth herself.

CHRISTINE

I know, A nun! How many of those do you still see around nowadays? But you already knew that. I swear to God Serdon, I won't have sex with you again, tonight or otherwise, unless you tell me how you did it. It was amazing.

> Projection of a group of three nuns looking down at them, all with Serdon's smiling mouth fades up

SERDON

Ah, what was so amazing?

CHRISTINE

There wasn't just one nun, there was a group of nuns shopping together, three of them.

SERDON

There are nuns everywhere.

CHRISTINE

Not like this; they were all really you, all of them at once, and you smiled at me. It was your smile but it was on all three of them at once, it was that smile you do when you come here, how did you do three people at once? All together next to one another?

The projection of the Three Nuns with Serdon's smile becomes a series of horror masks.

CHRISTINE

That's when I felt like throwing up. It was terrible. I ran from the store. Why are you doing all these terrible things to me? Francis, tell me, how did you do it and why are you doing it?

SERDON

Christine, this is all a really great story but can you snap out of it now? I want to have sex one more time before I leave, as you know my time here with you is quickly running out.

He puts his hand atop her, she moves it away.

CHRISTINE

Not yet, we can't have sex yet. I'll give you the extra time if you want it. I just need to tell you more.

He threw his hands up and rolled his eyes,

SERDON

There's more? Jesus! What else did I do? I had no idea that I am so amazing!

CHRISTINE

Oh yes, there's more. Lots more. The other day I caught you pretending to be my mother. I came in from the store and there you were, looking exactly like Thelma. And I said to you, "Serdon, how did you get in here? What have you done with my mother?" And you continued like you were worried about me and acted just like my mother does when she is all worried and you came and put your hand on my shoulder and said, "Calm down dear," just like she says sometimes. But I just shoved her hand and said, "Where is my real mother? Where?" And you said, "I am your real mother," and you told me again to just calm down. But what was I supposed to do? You had my real mother someplace else, under the house, or hidden back at your place, maybe in your garage.

SERDON

Jesus Christ Christine, where do you get all this?

CHRISTINE

Shut up, never mind, just listen! I'm not done, it was then I realized that if you could take over my own mother that you could take over me too, and if you took over me, then at least I'd know where the real people go when you take them over, so I said real loud, "Take me, Serdon! Take me, be me!" And you sat down after looking real wild-eyed and you just pretended to cry just like my mother cries when she's feeling helpless and lost and I shouted down at you while you were hunched over the kitchen table and I said, "What's the matter? You don't have the guts to be me? Come on, come on, be me," but you just kept on crying and you said to me, "Christine, my poor Christine, snap out of it," and you looked up at me with her face and it was too much, too much for me, so I pushed past and ran up here and got right into bed so I could "snap out of it."

> She closes her eyes and violently kneads her belly and her breasts. Serdon takes her by the wrist and stops her.

SERDON

Christine, open your eyes, stop playing with yourself like that, you're really turning me on. If you're not going to let me fuck you right now, just stop it!

> She opens her eyes and looks at his crotch.

CHRISTINE

I can see your funny little tent pole.

SERDON
Can we have sex now? That's what I came for, and I need to leave soon.

CHRISTINE
No not yet Francis, I want to know what you did with my Mother, and the Nuns, and the newspaper guy, and all those people, and I want to know it now. And the disguises, how did you do the three nuns at once? Listen, Francis, this is making me sick, why can't you tell me? Why can't you just be a normal person and come up to me in the store and be yourself and say hello, and how dare you do this to my Mother, that was the worst. Where did you learn to cry real tears when you were pretending to be my Mother? Tell me, Serdon. Tell me so I can feel better. Then, maybe then, we can think about fucking.

> Her hand moves towards his. He inches his hand towards hers.

SERDON
I am magic. That is how I manage to do it all. I am magic. OK Christine? Does that make you feel better?

> Their hands moved together.

CHRISTINE
You are telling me nothing, but I feel better, come here, It's time.

> They embrace under the blankets. Leandra circles the bed checking Serdon's hairline and face.

LEANDRA
How did he do it? I will get it out of him one day, he will tell me, I will make him tell me, I know how to make him tell me, I do. I know he was also the gas station attendant and the man behind the glass at the code enforcement bureau. I don't know how he is doing this, but he is. Green Boots, Green Boots, lying there dead

for decades high atop Everest. Funny how it all comes back to Everest, there are bodies on Everest, there are bodies on Everest even as I lay here, Everest is there and there are bodies on it, how do they climb the damned thing, how do they just go by all those damned bodies like some battlefield from the middle ages like one of those movies where there's a war and it's after a big battle is over; there are bodies laying around as far as the eye can see,

> He pushes harder into her; Leandra gets under the covers and joins them.

and the hero walks among the bodies and does what heroes do but the difference is there is moaning in the movie and there are half dead people; but on Everest they're all dead laying around as far as the eye can see and Serdon is all those dead bodies and the climbers reach the peak, the peak, the peak, the peak above the dead, high above the dead, they conquer the dead, but three nuns, three nuns, three nuns, how'd he do three nuns,

CHRISTINE

Three nuns!

SERDON

Why the hell did you yell three nuns?

> He buries his face in her hair and rolls off her. He gets out of bed and begins to dress.

CHRISTINE

You're good, Serdon, you're good at everything you do, so you are a master of disguises too. So what if you never tell me how or why you do it? Just don't do it anymore, OK? When I'm in the store be yourself and come up and give me a friendly hug and kiss, all right, don't watch me all sneaky like you do. It isn't necessary you know, it isn't really necessary. Do that stuff to other people. With

me you are fine to be yourself. You can come up and talk to me.
I might even like it if you were to say hi to me and recognize me
when we are away from this room. OK?

    Serdon nods as he dresses. He continues smiling at her. He
    takes out his wallet and tosses a fifty dollar bill on the bed.

SERDON
A bonus for tonight, next Thursday same time?

CHRISTINE
Yeah. Next Thursday, same time.

SERDON
OK bye. And I'll just be myself from now on, I promise. No
more disguises. If I see you, I'll be sure to come up and say Hi.
OK Christine?

CHRISTINE
OK. Bye. And thank you.

SERDON
No problem. Just don't worry about it anymore. Now go to sleep.

    Serdon starts to exit.

SERDON
My God, three nuns.

    Lights fade out, leaving a spot up on Serdon as
    he finishes dressing.

SERDON
I have no friends. I go to work every day, I see people there. They are
just paper cutouts moving around our make-believe, mock up of an

office where I work. My boss, telling me how well I'm doing, is a paper cutout. I walk the streets, I go to the store, stop to have a cup of coffee, the paper cutouts standing all around me with their fake smiles and their glinty eyes with their cups of coffee, their silent talk and their perfectly coiffed hair. I make my way through them, I always do. I go down to the creek and I climb back into the trusses, leaving my coffee on the creek bed below. And she is there, she is always there, blood and bone, flesh, and eyes, and hair, up in her little room, with her chair, and vanity in the corner, and her bed, in the center of all that filth. I understand that her mother fell apart after her Dad died in a truck accident, and that was when the place went to hell, there was nothing she could do about it.

I worry that she's going every bit a little more crazy, like tonight with all that talk about different disguises. Is she serious? I don't follow people around in disguises. If she is serious, she's not only at the edge; she's over the edge. Three nuns? Christine loves a good joke. But saying that I'm pretending to be different people, that I'm not who I am, that I'm not showing my true self, because that's what she's saying here. That's wrong, and Christine knows it.

> Light fades out. Lights fade up on the kitchen.

Christine and Leandra look out the kitchen door.

> Fade up Projection, stock footage of large yellow earth moving machines push over a house, leveling it.

THELMA (OFFSTAGE)

Christine! Christine,

> Thelma rushes into the kitchen clutching her robe around her. She suddenly grabs her throat with both hands and looks around in a panic.

Christine! Christine,

Christine and Leandra rush to her and put their arms
around her.

Christine!

CHRISTINE
Mom, Mom it's all right! It's all right!

Thelma's throws her arms around Christine

THELMA
Christine, I... It was awful they were tearing down the house they
didn't bother to inspect or anything they just came with big dirty
yellow machines and started tearing the place down, that's not
what they're going to do today is it, is it?

CHRISTINE
No. They're just looking at the place today. They're just looking, Mom.

End projection of large yellow earth moving
machines.

THELMA
Today's the day, right? Isn't it? The day we have to get out? Oh
my God... Oh my God!

CHRISTINE
No Mom. They're just looking at the place today. We talked about
this. We talked about this yesterday. They're just coming to look.

Thelma starts to panic.

THELMA
You know they're going to make us get out. You know that right?
They're going to make us get out.

Christine gently urged her back down.

                              LEANDRA
No, not today.

                              CHRISTINE
Mom. Not today. There's just a man coming to look. To look
and talk.

                              THELMA
Look and talk?

                        CHRISTINE/LEANDRA
Yes.

                              THELMA
That's all they're going to do, they're not going to tell us to get out?

                              CHRISTINE
Yes, that's all they're going to do today. Don't worry Mom.

                              THELMA
How will we live?

          Thelma wraps her arms around Christine and burrows
          into her.

                              LEANDRA
So where are we going to live, honey?

          Leandra begins to braid Christine's hair.

                              CHRISTINE
I don't know. I suppose I should start looking into that.

                              LEANDRA
They're bound to put us out after they see the place.

THELMA

How long after you fail the inspection do you have before you have to get out?

CHRISTINE

I don't know.

Leandra and Christine seat Thelma at the kitchen table.

LEANDRA

Ask the inspector today how long you have. But how will you find another place to live? How do you do that?

CHRISTINE

I guess we will cross that bridge when we come to it.

LEANDRA

I guess.

Thelma clears a space on the table, stacking the debris under the table.

THELMA

Look I cleared that space on the table, make sure you show the man how I cleared some space on the table. That's cleaning up right? Isn't that cleaning up?

CHRISTINE

Yes it is. I will show them, Mom. Hey listen, let me do the talking today OK? Don't say anything to the inspector.

THELMA

Why not?

CHRISTINE

Because I know what to say and we don't want to confuse them.

THELMA
You think I would confuse them?

CHRISTINE
No, no, not that. It's just it will be best if only one of us talks.

LEANDRA
Hey you know maybe we can charm the guy let him have a freebie upstairs that would make him happy.

CHRISTINE
Maybe if I do him, he'll pass the inspection, or even freebies for life, that's it. I'll give him freebies for life if he passes us!

Thelma forces a troubled smile.

THELMA
Don't joke that way Christine, you know I don't like it when you joke that way.

Thelma and Christine look into each other's eyes.

CHRISTINE
Well, I like it. This keeps us going Mom, this gets us through the days, a little funny stuff, you know, and some kindness from strangers. You are my mother and no matter what happens, I will protect you.

LEANDRA
This is why I was sent to you.

Christine and Leandra go to the kitchen door and look out. They return and sit at the kitchen table with Thelma.

CHRISTINE
The walkway is clear, you can get in, just like all the other men. So what if you can't see the lawn. Who needs lawns anyways?

Christine and Leandra smile as Thelma stares ahead blankly.

CHRISTINE/LEANDRA

Freebies for life.

Diana, a tall woman with blonde hair, wearing a yellow
hard hat, holding a clipboard, comes up to the door. She
looks at the clipboard and glances into the house and
back down at the clipboard.

LEANDRA

Damn it, no freebies.

Christine goes to the open door. Diana looks around
incredulously.

DIANA

Hello, are you Thelma Zidar?

CHRISTINE

No, That's my mother, she's inside.

Diana writes something quickly on the clipboard.

DIANA

Hi, my name is Diana.

Diana offers her hand; Christine shakes it.

CHRISTINE

Hello, I'm Christine Zidar.

DIANA

Did you know we were coming to inspect today?

CHRISTINE

Yes we did.

Diana looks back at the outside.

DIANA

It doesn't look like you cleaned up very much out here. What about inside? Did you clean up the inside?

CHRISTINE

I, uh, a little.

DIANA

Well let's see.

LEANDRA

Diana, isn't that the Goddess of the hunt? Or the Goddess of something, is Diana the Goddess of the hunt? Yes, she's the Goddess of the hunt and wild animals. Was she more than that? Later at night she's the Goddess of the moon. Right? And the Mountain Mother on cold slopes and the moon and Mt. Everest. Something funny in her knows, but...

Diana's tilts her head as she takes Christine's hand.

DIANA

Are you all right Miss Zidar? It looks a little like you might be coming down with something,

LEANDRA

In the clouds on the mountain, the freezing fog, and the moon.

CHRISTINE

Oh. No! I'm all right. Just sleepy I guess, I've been up all morning waiting for the inspection.

DIANA

Good, let's take a look then.

Christine ushers Diana in and around the stacked garbage.

DIANA

Is this safe?

CHRISTINE

Oh yes, it's all safe.

>Thelma looks at Diana and manages a sweet smile.

THELMA

Hello, you must be the inspector. I'm Thelma Zidar. This is my home, welcome.

>Diana extends her hand. They shake hands. Diana gets down to business.

DIANA

Hello, good to meet you, I'm Diana. Your daughter says you knew you were being inspected today. From what I can see you haven't cleaned much up,

>Martin's Projection (or Martin on stage) appears on the stage right wall. It peers down from above and behind bags of trash.

THELMA

We've done the best we can.

DIANA

Look at all this.

THELMA

This is my home!

LEANDRA

Goddess of the moon. You got to be kidding me.

Christine touches Thelma's arm.

CHRISTINE

Mom, remember what we said this morning.

THELMA

I know you said you would do all the talking but this is my home
and if she doesn't like my home well, I like it just fine,

Martin's Projection leans in and peers closely.

CHRISTINE

Mom!

Christine squeezes her mother's arm. Thelma quiets down.

DIANA

Which of you two work? Who's the breadwinner in this house?

THELMA

Martin was a contractor, my husband Martin.

Martin's Projection settles back.

CHRISTINE

Mother gets some money from her husband's social security and
she gets a small pension. But, I'm the breadwinner,

LEANDRA

She's going to ask.

DIANA

What do you do?

CHRISTINE

I'm a consultant. I run my own consulting business out of the house.

Leandra stifles a laugh; Christine cracks a smile.

DIANA

Consulting? What kind of consulting is it?

Martin's Projection turns, glowers and listens closely.

CHRISTINE

Diana, listen. I don't really see what these questions have to do with what you're here for today.

DIANA

This area is not zoned for commercial use, what kind of consulting do you do?

CHRISTINE

Counseling. I do marriage counseling.

Leandra laughs.

LEANDRA

Twisted. Very good, you pulled that right out of the air.

Thelma stares blankly. Diana writes on her clipboard.

DIANA

It's against the law to run a business from your house in this neighborhood. I have to look into this further, but I believe marriage counseling might be included.

CHRISTINE

You know, what happens today is all academic anyway, we've filed for an extension.

DIANA

You only get ten extensions. According to the records I have here, you've already had your ten.

She looks up from the clipboard, pencil poised.

CHRISTINE

We filed for another extension last week. They didn't say anything about a limit of ten.

DIANA

But let's not argue about that now. I'm here to inspect and from what I can see, you've made no effort to clean up. We're walking on trash and it stinks. Let's see the rest of the house.

They squeeze around the stacked trash and shuffle over the other trash.

DIANA

My God...

THELMA

This was clean. There are pictures. I can prove it somewhere in here someplace, there are pictures,

DIANA

You haven't done a thing. What's in there?

CHRISTINE

The dining room.

Diana stops, completely blocked by trash.

THELMA

We had Thanksgiving dinner and you could still see the crystal chandelier.

DIANA

Quite frankly, I've never seen anything this bad.

THELMA

But Martin died, don't you see.

DIANA

I've seen enough but I'm required to see the whole house.

> Christine leads the way around the trash. Diana, writes all over her clipboard. Thelma follows.

THELMA

There's a beautiful hardwood floor under there, there's a beautiful hardwood floor.

DIANA

That's nice,

THELMA

You ought to see it. We watched TV in there.

> Christine places a hand gently on Thelma.

> Martin's Projection fades out. The bedroom walls close back in.

CHRISTINE

Mom.

> Diana slips the clipboard under her arm and looks at Christine

DIANA

Upstairs, now please?

> Christine pushes aside bags of trash. They struggle up the stairs.

THELMA

Martin had birds up here; they laid eggs, fertile eggs with spots of blood.

> All at once Thelma nearly collapses. Christine catches her. Diana tries to negotiate her way around the garbage.

CHRISTINE

Haven't you seen enough? My mother is suffering.

DIANA

What's over there?

CHRISTINE

My room, that's my room.

DIANA

These stairs are a fire hazard.

LEANDRA

The men have no trouble with these stairs, why are you having trouble?

CHRISTINE

Come on. Come in. Look, and see.

> They all enter Christine's room. Thelma sits in the vanity chair.

DIANA

Why is this room so different from the rest of the house? It even smells good.

THELMA (PROUDLY)

This room is perfect just like my daughter.

> Leandra smiles and pokes Christine in the ribs, Christine flinches. Diana notices.

DIANA

What's wrong.

Christine frowns at Leandra.

CHRISTINE

Nothing, just an itch, I've got an itch.

LEANDRA (LAUGHS)

Marriage counseling!

DIANA

And can I see your office space?

CHRISTINE

Office space?

DIANA

Yes. You said you do counseling.

CHRISTINE

Oh, here, this is my office.

She points at the bed.

DIANA

But this is a bedroom.

CHRISTINE

We sit on the bed.

DIANA SUDDENLY SEES THE SITUATION CLEARLY.

DIANA

Oh.

CHRISTINE

It's friendly.

DIANA

This inspection is over; I'm afraid you have failed.

CHRISTINE

No. This inspection should never have happened. We've got an appeal in. This was supposed to happen next month; we just needed a little more time.

> Diana tries to leave. Christine gets in her way, trying to get her the change her mind.

DIANA

You have appealed ten times. That's the limit, you've had your time.

CHRISTINE

They said we could have one more appeal.

DIANA

You'll hear as to how we are going to proceed.

CHRISTINE

But…

DIANA

You have failed.

CHRISTINE

The Deputy Mayor…

DIANA

You have failed!

Diana pushes past Christine and weaves her way down the stairs. Thelma follows her.

LEANDRA

What did she say? Who is she to say anything?

THELMA

It was all sunshine and green grass. Then the police came and said Martin was hit by a truck. I worked in the dress factory!

Christine and Leandra pursue Diana down the stairs.

CHRISTINE

Get out of my house! Get out!

> The walls of Christine's room swing open. Fade up projection of the peak of Mt. Everest with dead bodies frozen on its slopes.

Diana leaves.

LEANDRA

Well I guess we told her.

THELMA

What dear, what did you say?

CHRISTINE

Nothing. Nothing at all, Mom.

> Christine and Leandra wrap their arms around each other and huddle together.

> Lights fade out followed by the projection fade out.

END ACT I

ACT II

Lights fade up on bedroom

Barry lies in Christine's bed, his hands folded across his ample stomach. Christine sits naked at the vanity brushing out her hair and listening. Leandra stands naked beside the vanity, brushing her hair, the strokes in unison with Christine as she looks back at Barry.

BARRY

You know, Christine, if only I had married you instead of my wife, if only I had known you before, years ago. What a pair we would have made, what a pair. Don't you think so Christine?

Christine and Leandra get into the bed.

CHRISTINE

You know you shouldn't lie to me, because I know.

BARRY

What? What do you know?

CHRISTINE

You know very well. You're really Bud from the gas station, So, how are you doing, Bud?

BARRY

Come on, cut it out Christine, it's spooky.

CHRISTINE

Did you know that this house is about to be condemned out from under me and my Mom? And you think you got it hard running a damned gas station? How would you like to be in me and Mom's shoes?

BARRY

Maybe you and your Mom should clean the place out.

CHRISTINE/LEANDRA

You know, you're just like a man to say a stupid thing like that!

BARRY

What?

CHRISTINE (SMILES)

Never mind, so tell me, how do you do it? Maybe I could do it too, but you men all do the craziest things and won't let me in on what you are doing or how to do it.

BARRY

Do what?

CHRISTINE

Bud, how do you switch places with Barry;

LEANDRA

Do you two do it a lot?

CHRISTINE

Could you switch back right now?

LEANDRA

Is it sexy, somehow,

CHRISTINE

Come on, be Barry.

LEANDRA

Not an old ugly thing like you, you know that's what you are, right? An old ugly thing who's inside of Barry.

CHRISTINE

But I really want to talk to Barry,

Barry puts his arm around her.

BARRY

Christine,

CHRISTINE

But I don't want to have sex with you, Bud. I want to be with Barry.

BARRY (SNAPS HIS FINGERS)

OK, here, now I'm Barry. Barry's back, OK?

CHRISTINE (STIFLING A LAUGH)

Prove to me you're Barry.

BARRY

How the hell am I supposed to do that?

CHRISTINE

Tell me something only Barry would know.

Christine's hand moves under the covers to Barry's groin.

BARRY

Oh, Christine, Barry knows that. Keep doing that.

CHRISTINE

What?

BARRY

Your hand, keep moving your hand like that.

CHRISTINE

How do you know you're not doing that with your own hand, I'm not doing anything with my hand.

BARRY

Because I have my hands right here, Oh my God, Christine!

> Christine suddenly springs from the bed, and holds up her semen covered hands.

CHRISTINE

Gross. You men are so damned gross. I need to go wash my hands.

BARRY

What?

> Christine goes into her bathroom. Leandra follows.

CHRISTINE

What did you do that for? You had my hand you moved my hand thank God he didn't see you. You made him come all over me.

LEANDRA

I did it for a joke. Oh come one, it was funny, you thought it was funny.

CHRISTINE

Funny? It was gross.

LEANDRA

This is my hand not yours.

CHRISTINE

No, this is mine.

LEANDRA

Mine.

CHRISTINE

Mine.

LEANDRA

Gross.

Christine slips on the bathrobe goes back in to Barry.

BARRY

Who were you talking to in there Christine?

CHRISTINE

Nobody.

She sits back on the vanity chair and resumes brushing her hair. Leandra comes out of the bathroom wearing her robe and leans back against the wall.

Don't do that anymore, OK?

BARRY

Do what?

CHRISTINE

Slime my hand like that. Your slime is very gross.

BARRY

It was your fault, you were the one rubbing me.

CHRISTINE

Let's not talk about it anymore.

BARRY

OK. But you brought it up.

CHRISTINE

No more talk.

BARRY

OK. Come here.

CHRISTINE

Why?

BARRY

I'm ready to go again.

She brushed harder.

CHRISTINE

We just did it twice, Bud. That's the deal.

She turns back to the mirror. Leandra puts her hand on Christine's shoulder.

LEANDRA

We should go away. I know I got you into this, but I think you should stop doing this stuff and we should go away somewhere.

CHRISTINE

We can't. There's mother.

BARRY

What are you talking to yourself in the mirror for?

Christine and Leandra turn to Barry.

CHRISTINE

Never mind Bud, this is none of your business. Just go to sleep. Take a nap.

LEANDRA

Or do something. You must be tired.

CHRISTINE

I need to talk to myself. I need to talk to myself the same way there's things you need to do to yourself.

> Barry rolled over in the bed and curls up. Christine turns to Leandra.

CHRISTINE

There, Bud won't talk to us again. Where were we?

LEANDRA

What happens to your mother when the house is condemned?

CHRISTINE (Deliberately.)

It can't get condemned.

LEANDRA

What if it does?

> Sound of the icy wind. The walls of the bedroom fold away. Fade up projection of the cold windblown peak of Mount Everest with dead, frozen bodies. A freezing cold overcomes Christine. Leandra pulls her close and warms her.

CHRISTINE

What about all those poor people down there; they thought they were going to be all right but then they got condemned by the ice and the snow and the wind and the cold and what did they do when they got condemned?

LEANDRA

They laid down and gave up and they came up here to heaven,

CHRISTINE

Yes heaven, they lay down and gave up and in their last mo-
ments they knew they were condemned the same way me and
my mother might be condemned and they probably thought of
God and of heaven.

LEANDRA

Or maybe they just thought about how God-damned cold it was.

CHRISTINE

But instead the cold probably froze their thoughts, and after a
while, before they actually died and I'm assuming that they did
die at peace, so to speak, put to sleep by the cold, except for those
who fell and are laying shattered in pieces, their deaths a little
more frightening, and they lay where they fell, they're probably
still laying there as we speak. What will freeze me and my mom's
thoughts when our house is condemned? Leandra, tell me. The ice
and the snow and the cold that comes when you know the worst
thing has happened and you don't know what you will do next,
but you know that you will be frozen in the ice, snow, and cold.
Like these people on this mountain must have known.

Sound of wind whipping up all around.

Christine strains to hear.

LEANDRA

All these people here are happy and free because for them there is nothing left and in nothingness there is happiness and freedom. When the
quest is over, everything these people ever wanted is fulfilled.

CHRISTINE

They are in their eternal sleep, and so the question becomes the
same, like, where do you go when you sleep? Or when you die?
What was there before you were alive is what there will be after

you die, both places are the same. But you can't remember any of it, that's what makes you scared, the part you can't remember.

LEANDRA

When this house gets condemned, you will return to that time that you can't remember, like those bodies on the mountain. Their souls are just lying there in that place. Not warm, not cold, not dark, not bright, but whatever was before. That's what's after, Christine.

CHRISTINE

No more thinking about quests, or inspections, or condemnations; that was all taken away from them by the freezing cold and the wind, way up here, taking their life. You know? Their souls are at peace.

> Christine and Leandra hold each other tight. They shiver from the blistering in the cold.

CHRISTINE

If we're lucky the appeal will take and we'll get Mom more time to clean up.

LEANDRA

You know that won't happen. She wants to keep everything buried. Your mother will never clean this place up. There are too many bodies. She likes the house frozen in time, just the way it is.

> The walls to Christine's room fold back in.

> Christine and Leandra release their embrace as Barry wakes up.

BARRY

Hey Christine. I dozed off, How about one last time before I go, I'm all rested up,

> Barry winks.

CHRISTINE

No, you've got to go now. You got your money's worth, and next time be yourself, be Bud. But if you want to know, you are not as much fun as Barry, tell Barry I said that. I had very little fun tonight. You had it all. You know?

BARRY

Yeah OK, whatever.

> Barry gets out of bed and rummaged through his clothes hung on the chair by the bed.

BARRY

Still, you're the greatest, Christine, a little weird maybe, but still the greatest.

CHRISTINE

Make sure Barry hears that. Be sure to tell him.

> Barry tosses the three hundred dollars to Christine and she counts it.

CHRISTINE

There's fifty dollars too much.

BARRY

A tip, a tip for all the laughs, you thinking I was Bud. What a laugh. You're a nut, Christine.

CHRISTINE

Don't come back as Barry again or I will surely kick you dead in the balls and you won't be good for nothing.

BARRY

Goodbye Christine.

CHRISTINE

Bye Bud,

> Barry goes out the door, clatters down the stairs and stumbles over some trash, walks past Thelma and out the door.

CHRISTINE

Well, here we are, just you and me, Leandra.

LEANDRA

Let's take a shower. He was dirty.

CHRISTINE

He's a mechanic.

LEANDRA

I thought you said he was the owner?

> Christine and Leandra pull off their robes and go into the bathroom.

> The sound of the shower begins.

CHRISTINE

Sending Barry on his way, imagine. Sending goddamned Barry on his fucking way. Sometimes it seems like they're all the same. They're all filthy, all of them.

> Sound of the shower stops.

> Christine and Leandra come out of the bathroom, toweling vigorously. They dry each other's backs.

CHRISTINE

But sometimes they're all clean, just like snowflakes. Beautiful…

> Christine and Leandra crawl into bed and under the blankets.

> The bedrooms walls fold out. Projection of the frozen slopes of Mount Everest with its dead bodies fades up.

LEANDRA
Honed razor sharp by the fierce winds whipping over the slopes.

CHRISTINE
Melting, but not for long. Then freezing as the wind pushes the water away leaving a razor edge, like the icy peaks of Mount Everest. The slopes and the frozen bodies.

> They snuggle down deep into the bed and peek out from under her covers and gaze at the windswept slope of Everest.

LEANDRA
Icy and windswept.

CHRISTINE
Today and tomorrow and the tomorrow after that and the tomorrow after that swirling in ice white fog.

LEANDRA
Until the freezing breath shouts.

> Christine and Leandra pull the blankets tightly around them.

CHRISTINE (WHISPERS)
Before we were born there was nothing, wonderful nothing. Nothing, like death must actually be; all those bodies just lying there in nothingness,

LEANDRA
Knowing that if there was a God he would never allow it to happen.

Lights fade out. Spot fades up on Barry.

Barry fidgets nervously.

BARRY

I do worry about Christine going off the deep end. One time I went to see her and she said "I'm a dead person today. Would you fuck me even though I am a dead person? I said, "What the hell are you talking about?" and she started waving her hands real crazy and started explaining how she had some kind of syndrome that made her believe she was dead. I said how can you be dead and know that you have some kind of syndrome that makes you think you are dead? She fell on the bed and played dead that whole night. So I did her, limp like that. She never moved, never made a sound. I felt really weird. It even started smelling a little like a funeral home. But I knew that was just in my head, and it meant I had to get the hell out of there. I think I'm going to have to stop seeing Christine pretty soon because she's really getting stranger and stranger.

Light fade out. Lights fade up on the kitchen.

Thelma sits in her chair at the table staring blankly ahead.

TV flickering reflects from Thelma's face. Sound of a knock at the door.

Thelma quickly looks to the door but turns away and resumes her blank stare.

The knock sounds again.

Thelma jerks her head toward the door and back again.

The knock repeats.

Thelma gets up from her chair and steps toward Christine's room.

THELMA (SOFTLY)

Christine! Christine, come down, I need you.

Lights fade up on Christine's room.

Christine and Leandra cozily lie in bed next to each other.

THELMA

Christine!

Christine gets out of bed puts on a red robe and comes halfway down the stairs

Sound of knocking the stage right side wall swings open.

CHRISTINE

Mom, someone's knocking. Answer the door.

Martin's Projection looks down into the kitchen.

THELMA (AFRAID)

I can't answer the door. Nobody knocks on my door at ten in the morning. I've never answered the door at ten in the morning before.

The knocking continues more insistently

Christine comes down passes by her Mother and goes to the door.

CHRISTINE

Well, we've got to get it, what if it's important?

THELMA

What could be so important?

CHRISTINE

We'll see,

Christine pushes trash aside and opens the door. The pasty white face of the Process Server, a small man in a white short sleeved shirt and short black tie appears in the doorway. He holds a briefcase with a blue folder sticking out.

PROCESS SERVER

Are you Thelma Zidar?

> Process Server looks past Christine into the terrible state of the room beyond.

CHRISTINE

No, no I'm not. Mom! This is for you, there's a man here to see you.

> Thelma retreats to the far corner of the kitchen.

THELMA

I, I can't come to the door I'm not dressed,

CHRISTINE

Well you were dressed a minute ago, come to the door.

> Christine turns back to the Process Server.

CHRISTINE

I'm sorry about this.

PROCESS SERVER

That's OK, do you live here?

CHRISTINE

Yes. I'm Chrstine Zidar. I'm Thelma's daughter. What is this all about?

> Process Server takes a notice from the blue folder and hands it to her.

PROCESS SERVER

Here. Here's a notice from the Thayer County Sheriff's office. A copy is also being mailed to you. I can leave this with you, what's your name again? I need to write down who I leave this with.

> Christine takes the notice. Process server whips a form out of his folder.

> CHRISTINE

Christine Zidar.

> Process Server squints at the folder as he writes her name.

> PROCESS SERVER

That's an eviction notice and notice of condemnation from the county. I was told your house was inspected a week ago. Is that right?

> CHRISTINE (CAUGHT OFF GUARD.)

What? Eviction notice? When?

> Process Server hands her the notice. Christine reads it.

> PROCESS SERVER

Your house failed inspection and is being condemned as a health and safety hazard. Here, step aside, I need to tack this note to the door.

> He reaches into his briefcase and produces a push pin. He takes a yellow sheet of paper out of the folder. Christine moves quickly, takes it from his hand.

> CHRISTINE

"Condemned." No, you're not hanging that sign on my Mother's door.

> Christine pushes it back in his face,

> PROCESS SERVER

OK fine, then you do it.

> Process Server pushes the notice back towards her, then pushes the tack into the door frame. Thelma steps out of the corner toward the door.

> Martin's Projection stoops down. His eye peers through the kitchen door

> THELMA (WEAKLY)

What is it?

CHRISTINE

Mom, never mind, go back inside. I'll tell you later,

PROCESS SERVER

You've been served, have a nice day. I need to write down who I leave this with. And be out by that date.

The Process Server turns and leaves.

Martin's projection fades out.

Christine closes the door, goes to Thelma and takes her hand.

CHRISTINE

Mom, this is a notice from the county. They want us out in a week.

THELMA

Jesus Christ. Save us, Jesus Christ!

Thelma's eyes roll back; she falls to the floor, tries to get up but collapses. Christine's turns and throws open the door and waves the condemnation notice.

CHRISTINE

Help! Sir! Help, help!

The Process Server comes running back.

PROCESS SERVER

What's wrong? Are you all right; what's wrong?

CHRISTINE

My Mother has collapsed, Call 911, do you have a phone?

The Process Server rushes in the door and sees Thelma lying there. He whips out his cell phone and punched in 911, kneels next to Thelma and feels around her neck for a pulse.

He tears the notice from Christine's hand looks at it as he urgently speaks into the cell phone.

PROCESS SERVER

Yes, I need an ambulance right away at 445 Pickwick. A woman has collapsed. She's not moving, 445 Pickwick. Yes I think there's a pulse. Send an ambulance quick!

Martin's Projection looks down from the bedroom wall.

The Process Server hands the cell phone to Christine.

PROCESS SERVER

They want to talk to you.

Christine takes the phone as the Process server begins CPR on Thelma.

The sound of distant siren fades in

CHRISTINE

Yes? I'm her daughter. Thelma Zidar. Yes that's her. I am Christine Zidar, him? He came from the county, he served us a notice and she collapsed. An eviction notice. Yes she took one look at it and collapsed. Yes. Yes I will.

The sound of the siren fades grows louder.

The Process Server frantically continues CPR on Thelma,

The siren pulls up and suddenly stops.

Two paramedics rush up with their equipment.

CHRISTINE

Yes, they're here, yes. OK I'm hanging up.

Two paramedics wheel in a gurney and their equipment.

PARAMEDIC 1

Where?

> They look around, their mouths drop open as they see the state of the kitchen. They push their way to Thelma.

PARAMEDIC 2

We'll take over now, step back let us see her.

> Paramedic 1 slips an oxygen mask on Thelma. Paramedic 2 looks around the room, amazed.

PARAMEDIC 2

You guys live here?

PROCESS SERVER

No, not me. I just work for the county.

CHRISTINE

I live here. She's Thelma Zidar and I'm her daughter.

> Christine is suddenly woozy; she steadies herself on the table.

PROCESS SERVER

You all right Ma'am? You look sick.

> Christine shoves the notice in the Process Server's face.

CHRISTINE

Wouldn't you be? Beside this is all your fault! Look at my Mother. It's your fault, you and your goddamned notice!

PROCESS SERVER

I, I'm just doing my job.

CHRISTINE

Look at my Mother!

PARAMEDIC 1

Step aside, step aside. Do people really live here?

> The Paramedics lift Thelma onto the gurney.

CHRISTINE

Where are you bringing her; which hospital?

PARAMEDIC 2

General, step aside; come on I have the gurney,

> Thelma suddenly sits straight up and tears the oxygen mask from her face. Paramedic 1 tries to put it back. She pushes him away.

THELMA

No!

> Everyone freezes and stares at Thelma

THELMA

No one is taking me from this house! I'm not going to the hospital, I just fell down. I fall down, what's wrong with that? Don't you ever fall down? Do you kick a woman out of her house like you're doing just because she falls down? I'm seventy-five, I have a right to fall down!

> Christine goes to her.

CHRISTINE

Mom? Mom, are you OK?

> Thelma waves her arms and makes her way to the kitchen table.

THELMA

Of course I'm OK, wouldn't you fall down too if you saw you were being thrown out of your house? Well it said that we have time, so you're not taking me anywhere today just because I fell down, we still have time, the piece of paper says that we still have time, so I'm staying right here, right in my home!

Martin's Projection smiles, at Thelma from the opened bedroom wall.

Thelma struggles to her feet, Paramedic 1 tries to steady her by the arm but she pulls away. He steps back into a stacked pile of trash, it tumbles over, falling around them.

THELMA

Don't touch me! Everybody, everybody, get out of my house! Leave me and Christine alone!

PARAMEDIC 1

All right ma'am, but, are you sure you're all right,

THELMA

Yes! Just a little tingly in the hands. Get out!

Christine helps Thelma to her chair at the kitchen table. Thelma sits; Christine turns to the Process Server.

CHRISTINE

And tell your damned cronies down at the borough hall that there's no way we're leaving this house, you tell them that.

PROCESS SERVER

I can't tell them that Ms. Zidar there's an appeals process; you need to come down to the county and there are forms that you need to fill out and…

Christine waves her hand across his face.

CHRISTINE

Shut Up! Never mind! Just never mind! Never mind the process!
Never mind the county! Never mind the forms! We're not leaving, now everyone get out!

THELMA

Go on, get out! Get out!

> Paramedic 1 and 2 retreat out of the house

PROCESS SERVER

Remember, a copy of the notice will come in the mail. It will
outline the appeals process.

> Christine follows the Process Server as he leaves. She
> stands boldly at the door and slams it shut.

CHRISTINE

Jesus Mom, that was some way to start the day.

THELMA

I'm not leaving my house. They came to take me from my house
but I'm not leaving.

CHRISTINE

You don't have to Mom. You don't have to. But are you really
OK? You fell pretty hard there.

> Martin's Projection stands impassive; watching.
> Christine gets up and wipes a strand of hair from
> Thelma's face.

THELMA

I'm just a bit sore, I'm sure everything is going to be all right.

> Christine hugs Thelma to her.

CHRISTINE

I love you, Mom.

THELMA (MUTTERING)

They don't have to look at our house when they came out of theirs, there are other houses in the neighborhood, why do they have to focus on ours. Busybodies.

> Christine sees the crumpled up eviction notice lying near the front door. She goes to pick it up.

CHRISTINE

We had better not lose that piece of paper. It's important. Imagine living in a house with a CONDEMNED sign tacked to the door, like that man had wanted us to do? Condemned is a horrible word! A horrible word!

> Christine takes the crumpled eviction notice and places it atop a pile of other garbage.

CHRISTINE

For safekeeping. Just like everything else is in the house for safekeeping, right mother?

THELMA

It is important to keep things in order; it's like keeping pieces of yourself, and if anything is gone, we wouldn't be whole; and we would die. I would die living any other way.

CHRISTINE

Mom, what are we going to have for breakfast,

THELMA

I, I really shouldn't have anything at all, my stomach is in such knots, but one must eat, mustn't one?

CHRISTINE

Yes. Maybe some toast?

> Christine and Thelma stay seated at the table

>> The second wall to Christine's bedroom swings
>> open. Fade up projections of the slopes of Mt.
>> Everest.

> Leandra enters the bedroom.

LEANDRA

The mountain will always protect you.

>> Lights slowly fade out on the kitchen.

> Christine goes up to her bedroom. She and Leandra strip
> off their robes. Christine goes into her bathroom. Leandra
> goes to the window and stands there.

>> Sound of water running. Cross fade to projection
>> of the peak of Mount Everest with the bodies
>> strewn about. Fade in sound of the wind. Fade
>> out the sound of the water.

> Christine joins Leandra. They stare out the window then
> turn to each other.

CHRISTINE

Mack's here.

LEANDRA

The beautiful icy mountain, but there are only two ways down
from the peak; the hard way or start the easy way and fail.

>> Christine crosses to the vanity. Mack enters and gets into
>> bed. He has a toothpick and works on his teeth. Christine
>> looks back at Mack through the vanity mirror. Leandra
>> comes to Christine and stands beside her.

CHRISTINE

Mack, who do I look like? Be honest.

> Mack puts the toothpick on the bedside table and runs his hands through his thick gray hair.

MACK

You look like your big, beautiful self.

CHRISTINE

No I don't. I'm a brunette. When I look in the mirror, I'm some blonde with an ugly skinny face and no lips. Come here, come here and look in this mirror.

> He gets out of the bed and crosses to the mirror. He looks in it with her. Leandra studies Mack.

MACK

OK? Now what?

CHRISTINE

Who do you see?

MACK

I see you.

CHRISTINE

Well, I see a stranger! A skinny, ugly stranger. Oh, no help from you.

> Christine grabs Mack and pulls him to her. She buries her face in his shoulder.

MACK (WHISPERS)

Oh Christine. That's nonsense. But here. Here,

> He warmly embraces her rocks her like a baby.

Want to have another go. I'm ready.

CHRISTINE
No, you need to tell me why I look that way in the mirror first. I must look the way I see myself in that mirror. Look at me Mack. What do I look like?

MACK (IMPATIENTLY.)
You look like yourself Christine.

CHRISTINE
Yes and how is that? Describe me.

MACK
But you know what you look like,

CHRISTINE
Describe me!

MACK
You have brown hair, brown eyes, high cheekbones, pretty lips, a cute nose, you're a pretty girl.

CHRISTINE
You're lying. I'm a skinny blonde bitch with missing buck teeth.

MACK
You have perfect teeth and you're not skinny or blonde,

CHRISTINE
Why are you lying to me Mack? Why won't you tell me the truth? What's wrong with you? Tell me what's wrong with you, that you can see that?

She sits back down on the vanity chair and holds her face in her hands.

MACK

I, no, there's nothing wrong with me Christine,

He steps up and put his hand on her shoulder. She shrugs herself violently away.

CHRISTINE

Yes there is. You're not seeing me right. Why won't you tell me what you see?

She began to cry and Mack stepped back and looked at her.

MACK (QUIETLY)

What's the matter with you? You are so smart, so alive, so good in bed, but so afraid of God knows what. I don't know how to help you Christine. I'm so sorry. But I just don't know.

Mack turned from her and returned to the bed and lay back down, pulled the sheet over himself, he pats the mattress beside him.

Christine, Christine come here. Let's do it again. I'm paying you for this time, you know that right?

She turned her head toward him while remaining hunched over the vanity top.

CHRISTINE

What do you see when you look in the mirror. Do you see yourself the way you think you look?

MACK

Of course I do. Come here, Christine.

CHRISTINE

Maybe you don't look the way you think you look. How do you think you look, Mack? Tell me and I'll tell you if that's what I see.

MACK

Christine, this is stupid. Cut it out. Come here,

CHRISTINE

No, tell me!

MACK (Smiles.)

OK, I'm a handsome, blue-eyed, grey-haired, old man. Does that match what you see?

CHRISTINE

So far. What kind of lips do you have? What kind of nose?

MACK

I have, I guess I have thin lips and a fairly big nose. Come on Christine, this is stupid.

CHRISTINE

No! It's not stupid!

She turns and buries her face in her hands. Mack starts picking his teeth again.

MACK

Christine, I paid you three hundred dollars. Now, come here and earn that money. Forget all this mirror shit. You look like yourself, OK? You look good. Come on. My dick is hard!

Her face still buried.

CHRISTINE

No. I am too ugly. I need to quit this business I am too ugly to arouse any man.

MACK

You've got me all worked up. Look.

> He pointed to the lump in the sheet where his erection stands waiting. She glances over, smiles suddenly, gets up and goes to the bed.

CHRISTINE

OK, since you paid I must be good enough for you.

> She gets into the bed next to him and stares up at the ceiling.

CHRISTINE

Did you know that they're trying to put me and my mother out of the house? They served us with an eviction notice the other day. I threw it on the trash. They wanted to put a condemned sign on our door. I wouldn't let them. This is my room. This should always be my room. They can't just throw an old woman and her grown daughter on the street, can they Mack?

> She listens for his answer without looking down from the ceiling.

MACK

No, of course not. They've got to give you time. They've got to give you a chance to find another place.

CHRISTINE

But there's a date on it. It's next week.

MACK

The date means nothing. They just got to put some date down so they pull it out of the air. You just have to go down to the county and work it all out. You're going down to the county, right Christine? To work it all out?

CHRISTINE

I, I don't know. Fuck the process and the appeals.

MACK

Well, you should. They'll give you time. They don't want people in the street or living out of their cars or anything like that.

CHRISTINE

Oh, I think they do, Mack. I don't think they give a shit about anybody. Oh, Mack, I don't know what we're going to do.

He raised himself on his elbow and looked at her.

MACK

Yes you do. You're going to go to the county and work it out.

She pulls her hand from his and looks away.

CHRISTINE

Everything is crazy Mack. I'm seeing things, I'm hearing things. Did I tell you that last night I was up half the night because the baby who lives under us wouldn't stop screaming?

MACK

What? What baby?

CHRISTINE

You heard me, there's a baby living somewhere under us.

MACK

Christine, listen. There's nobody living under you. This is not an apartment,

> Leandra abruptly appears in the door. She reached out her arms. Christine rolls toward her.

CHRISTINE

Leandra, come to me my love!

MACK

What are you saying? Who are you talking to, are you talking to me?

> Leandra sits on the bed smiling. She takes Christine's hand.

CHRISTINE

Hush.

MACK

What?

CHRISTINE

I said hush. I, I know we don't live in an apartment, like you said. Does that make you feel better? I know that. I imagine the baby. OK? Does that make you feel better?

> Leandra smiles over both of them

But I know what's happening with that mirror. That's not me I'm seeing in the mirror. That's somebody else.

MACK

But who were you talking to just then?

Christine and Leandra exchange glances.

CHRISTINE

Never mind that. I feel better now. I know I look like myself.
That's just someone else in the mirror. Hey maybe I got here some
kind of magic mirror, Mack go look in the vanity mirror and see
who you see.

MACK

Christine, this is crazy.

CHRISTINE

Go on. Do it.

He throws back the sheet and crosses to the vanity wearing only his socks. Leandra and Christine share a smile.
Mack looks into the mirror.

MACK

I see myself Christine. I see myself so I must not have the same
problem you do.

CHRISTINE

I have no problem, what problem?

MACK

I uh, no, no problem. Christine, I think I am going to go now. I
think you earned your money tonight.

Leandra frowns at Christine; Christine frowns at Mack.

CHRISTINE

What? No. It's only nine o'clock. You get another hour. I don't
want to be...

She paused. He looks at her as he pulls on his clothes. .

MACK

What, what don't you want?

CHRISTINE

I don't want to be alone. Please stay, tell you what. I'll give you the whole rest of the night free.

MACK

You got me spooked Christine. You talk about the mirror, you talk to yourself, you tell me that you hear babies crying at night. I'm going to leave. Just try to get some sleep. I think that should help.

Leandra and Christine frown at one another.

CHRISTINE

We could make it a threesome, if you stay, we can make it a threesome. For free.

He stops getting dressed.

MACK

What? You'd get another girl to come in?

Leandra laughs.

CHRISTINE

Yes! That's what I'll do. I'll get another girl to come in. Will you stay?

MACK

What will I have to pay?

CHRISTINE

I said it's for free.

MACK

OK, do it.

                         CHISTINE
Do what?

        Leandra looks on and smiles.

                          MACK
Call the other girl. Is she clean?

                        CHRISTINE
Oh yes. Very clean.

        She squeezes Leandra's hand under the sheet.

                          MACK
OK, let's do it.

        She glances at Leandra. Leandra gets up and crosses to
        Mack. She massages his shoulders, kisses the back of his
        neck, and presses hard against him.

                        CHRISTINE
OK, there you go.

        Leandra wraps her arms around Mack, squeezes hard and
        lets go.

                          MACK
What do you mean, there you go? Who's here? I don't see anyone here.

                        CHRISTINE
I'm here, come to me, while we wait for her.

                          MACK
But you haven't made any calls.

CHRISTINE

Oh no, I arranged for this as a surprise for you. Isn't it your birthday soon? Isn't it?

MACK

No.

Leandra blows into Mack's ear.

CHRISTINE

Well I thought it was, you've been such a good customer I thought I'd give you a surprise, she'll be here any time now. That's why you shouldn't leave, but let's not waste my time or your money, come here, take off those pants and all that other stuff that you've got on underneath and come here to me!

Leandra tears at his shirt, rips open his pants

MACK

All right

Mack slips under the covers. Leandra clings to him Christine rolls over and puts her arms around Mack. The two women writhe over him on the bed.

CHRISTINE

How do you like us Mack, huh? How do you like us?

MACK

What? Who's us?

CHRISTINE

Us. Me. I am two women. I am three women. I am fifty, a hundred women all over you. Maybe a million women, Mack. Maybe all the women in the world, or the universe!

> Leandra and Christine laugh and swarm over Mack. He is overwhelmed.

MACK

Where's the other girl? What universe? Where,

CHRISTINE

Here! We are all here! Just for you.

> Mack shudders, moans and closes his eyes. Christine gets off him, Leandra lies her head on Mack's shoulder and smiles. Mack breathes heavily. He opens his eyes.

MACK

Oh God,

CHRISTINE

God what?

MACK

God, you're good. You talk crazy but you are good.

> Leandra rolls off Mack, gets out of bed and goes into the bathroom.

CHRISTINE

Now there's just the two of us Mack. And I'm done for the night. So get out.

MACK

What about the other?

CHRISTINE

Get out! I have gone off duty! Get out!

Christine gets up and goes to the mirror. She looks at the stranger who looks back at her. Mack quietly gets up, gets dressed, places a fifty dollar tip on the bed and leaves without saying a word, but all the while staring at her babbling into the mirror.

CHRISTINE

I am not afraid of you anymore. I'm not afraid of you or anyone else that pretends to be me. You are not me. You are a stranger. I am me and you are not we are not all here together. You won't trick me anymore, I can see it in your eyes, I will not be fooled again.

Mack leaves. When the door closes behind him, she brings her hands to her face, looks at the door, squints at the mirror, and laughs.

Lights fade out. Lights fade up on Mack.

MACK

I was in prison for five years for selling pills that I got from a buddy who was a pharmacist. My dad died while I was doing my time. It also ended up killing Mom because she couldn't stand to be alone without him. She lasted six months after Dad died. Everyone says that she died of a broken heart. She just coasted her life to an end, just like when you are in a car and you shut it off and throw it in neutral and it just slowly, slowly, coasts to a stop. The engine ain't running any more. Her engine shut off when they closed Dad's coffin. You could see it in her face. She was switched off from that point on.

She tells me that sometimes she goes out on the roof. She tells me some shit about its Mount Everest out there. About how people died there and just stay where they fell forever. It fascinates her. Why do people want to climb the damn thing if all they are going to be doing is stepping over the dead people that fell before them?

The place is very creepy, she says, like a big ice cream sundae with dead ants sprinkled all on top! Christine's mother believes that the garbage is the ghost of her dead husband. She says these things when she goes into that trance she does when she sits in front of that mirror on the vanity.

Christine's really getting more and more bizarre. Bizarre people like that end up doing bizarre things, like all of a sudden pulling out a gun and going, "OK, the person in the mirror has just told me to kill you." And I'd end up taking a bullet or two for her craziness. Now, don't get me wrong, I don't think Christine would actually do this, but I sense that sometimes she's hearing voices or seeing things that aren't there. So she may end up taking the advice of one of her voices. She may end up plugging a bullet or two into me if her voices tell her to.

> Lights fade out on Mack. The bedroom walls swing open. A Projection fades up of an empty lot where the house used to be, surrounded by two homes with well manicured lawns. Lights fade up on Christine and Leandra sitting on the bed.

LEANDRA
Condemned houses, rotten beyond repair get torn down and all that remains is a grassy space. The city takes over and the grassy space briefly becomes a memorial to what happened.

CHRISTINE
But they'll rebuild a house here right? Being the house of a hoarder doesn't make it an infamous house.

> They join hands.

CHRISTINE
Who's going to come? What will they do?

> Christine grabs the bedspread and squeezes.

LEANDRA

They may come with sirens blazing and force us out of the house and then where will we live, where will we go?

Sound of a knock at the door.

Christine abruptly gets up.

Lights fade up on the house as

Christine goes to the door.

CHRISTINE

Did I tell Lewis we'd be at this Motel tonight?

Christine opens the door. Lewis stands there.

CHRISTINE

Glad to see you. Lewis has come early again. I must have told you.

Lights fade out in the house and the walls close.

Lewis follows her to the bedroom.

LEWIS

Must have told me what?

CHRISTINE

Oh nothing. You're here. In the right place. And at the right time. That's what counts. Come on in. Well, how do you like the new place.

LEWIS

I, what do you mean new place?

She looks puzzled and tilts her head.

CHRISTINE

I don't mean anything Lewis. Come on. Fork it over.

He smiles as he takes out his wallet.

                          LEWIS
You little devil.

          He pulls out three hundred dollars, and lays it on her dresser.

                        CHRISTINE
Did you have trouble finding the place?

                          LEWIS
I've come here a hundred times. What do you mean?

                        CHRISTINE
I don't know why, that just came out. Come on Lewis. Clothes off.
Let's get down to our business.

                          LEWIS
That's my Christine.

          He takes off his clothes, turns around and drapes them
          over her chair. Christine gets under the sheets while his
          back is turned. Lewis gets into bed with her and Chris-
          tine goes to work on him.

                    Fade up voices of people in adjoining motel
                    rooms having sex.

                    Tanady's VOICE moans.

                    TANADAY'S VOICE
Ooooh. Oooh. Ooooh yes, yes.

                        CHRISTINE
Oooh, in the room above, you are good! You are really, really good!

                        CHRISTINE
Did you hear that Lewis? Did you hear those other people having
sex in the room above?

LEWIS
What? There's no room above yours.

CHRISTINE
Oh! I know. I don't know why I said that! Silly me,

> They stretch out under the sheets. Christine suddenly sits up.

> Voices and sounds come from the motel room next door.

> Christine cocks her head and listens. She recognizes the voice.

SERDON'S VOICE
I usually go to Christine Zidar, but you are so different, so much more tender, so much calmer, someone I can really talk with, I like it.

WOMAN'S VOICE 1
Sure, I know about Christine. She was in the nut house for years. Did you know that?

BARRY'S VOICE
I knew she was in the hospital but you say it was the nut house?

WOMAN'S VOICE 2
Sure.

BARRY'S VOICE
What exactly was wrong with her?

WOMAN'S VOICE 2
I don't know but she was in there for a long time. Everybody who's been to see her says she's nuts.

> Christine jumps from bed, pulls her arm back and is about to pound on the wall when Leandra holds her back.

LEANDRA

Christine, don't do it,

CHRISTINE

But don't you hear what they are saying about me? That's a client of mine that's talking over there, talking about me.

LEANDRA

Don't bang the wall and don't yell! You'll spook Lewis!

Christine relaxes.

LEANDRA

What difference does it make what your clients think of you as long as they come back every week and you get your three hundred dollars and they get their good honest fuck, that's what counts. Remember, that's not a man lying out there that's a three hundred dollar bill. What they think is meaningless.

Christine washes her hands and listens to the wall, but there was silence now. She turns and goes to Lewis. He lay smiling on the bed, one knee up, hands behind his head. She stares for a moment.

LEWIS

What? What's wrong?

The wall above the bed suddenly got her attention.

SOUND of Voices come from behind the thin motel wall.

Christine looks past Lewis who waits for an answer.

BARRY'S VOICE

I know. Yeah, I know.

CHRISTINE

It's Barry. Lewis!

LEWIS

What?

Christine raises her hand to her ear.

CHRISTINE

No. Let me listen.

BARRY'S VOICE

Yeah, Christine Zidar was my other whore but I think I like you better, come on let's do it again, a growing boy like me got's to do it again,

CHRISTINE

No!

Christine bounds over Lewis and forces him to leap from the bed.

No!

Christine slams her open hand against the wall above the bed.

SOUND of hollow, thundering knocks. VOICES finally stop.

Christine kneels on the bed, breathing heavily.

LEWIS

Christine, Christine, are you all right? What the hell did you do that for? I'm getting out of here, you really are nuts this time,

Lewis gets dressed quickly.

CHRISTINE

No, don't go Lewis, I just needed to shut them up.

LEWIS

Shut who up? Who? No. This is enough. Step aside, let me get my things.

CHRISTINE

The voices in the next room, no Lewis, no, you can't leave; I'll be all alone.

Christine tears at her hair as he struggles into his clothes.

CHRISTINE

Lord God no, don't go, you are the one I like the best, you are the one I like to talk to, stay, please stay.

He looks at her.

LEWIS

I'd love to stay Christine, but you scare me. You scared the hell out of me, what voices? What voices are you talking about?

CHRISTINE

The people all around us in all the other rooms!

LEWIS

There are no other rooms! This is your house! Listen.

He puts his hands on her shoulders and looks into her eyes.

LEWIS

Don't cry Christine, just calm down all right? I'll stay a while, but let me get dressed now. I don't want to have sex any more tonight but I'll stay a while if that will make you happy. All right? Here, over there, go over there and put your clothes on too. Let's, let's just relax a while. OK?

CHRISTINE

OK.

They get dressed. Christine sits on her vanity chair and Lewis sits on the bed. They are silent. She looks over at Lewis as if she can see right through him.

CHRISTINE

How is your wife? How is she doing these days?

LEWIS

My wife is fine. Same old, same old.

They cracked smiles.

CHRISTINE

Still got the same job?

LEWIS

Oh yeah, you know, that old job, if I did something as radical as change jobs I'd tell you, you know that. You're my girl, Christine.

CHRISTINE

Your girl? What do you mean, I'm your girl? You said, "My girl."

LEWIS

You're my girl, a good friend. Why are your hands shaking Christine? What's the matter?

She sits up straight and raises her head.

CHRISTINE

I feel like a piece of meat, Lewis. It really hit me tonight here in this motel,

He rolls his eyes.

CHRISTINE

If I disappeared tomorrow you could find a new whore to fuck, snap, just like that.

She snaps her fingers.

LEWIS

Christine, listen. First off, I'll tell you why you worry me. You say we're in a motel. But this is no motel room. We are in your house, in your room, like we always are. And second,

CHRISTINE

No! We are at the Half Moon motel. Thank God I got out of that house. This motel room is much better.

He raised a hand and simply continued talking calmly and evenly.

LEWIS

We've been seeing each other for a while, I think about you often and I think of you as a friend. I worry about you Christine.

Leandra continues to sit by her on the bed.

LEANDRA

You are with me.

CHRISTINE

Yes but that all is coming to an end now.

LEWIS

What? What did they do to you in that hospital to make you do the things you do and say the things you say? First off, who were you just talking to? There's no one there.

Christine sits up.

CHRISTINE

I was talking to my friend, Leandra.

LEWIS

Leandra? There's just us two here.

CHRISTINE

No, Leandra is also here with us. Leandra is everywhere all the time.

He looked around the room.

SOUND of Mack's voice through the wall.

MACK'S VOICE

I see Christine Zidar too, but she's not like you. You're a lot better. I think I'll just see you from now on, I think I'll just see you, she's just a piece of meat to me, I don't really care about her.

Christine claps her hands over her ears, stands and stamps on the floor.

CHRISTINE

Shut up! Shut up!

Lewis rises and grabs his jacket,

LEWIS

I had better go, goodbye Christine,

Christine stamps the floor. Lewis exits.

SOUND OF VOICE stops as the door closes.

Leandra takes Christine by the arm.

CHRISTINE

Why am I cursed? Why do I have such an awful life, Leandra? Lewis, where's Lewis, he ran out didn't he? Will he be coming back? He didn't say he was coming back like he usually does,

She throws her arms around Leandra.

The voices of all her John's cascade as the bedroom walls swing open. Projections of the windswept slopes of Mt. Everest and its dead cold bodies in the ice come at her through swirling wind.

VOICES

There are things you can do. There are things you would be good at... You've got to get out of here. Get a job and take care of your mother. Quit this business. You need a legitimate job. You need to help your mother... Go... your mother... Go help your mother!

LIGHTS FADE UP on the kitchen.

Christine runs down to Thelma. Thelma wakes in the reclining chair that she always sleeps in. The Process Server comes gently through the door.

PROCESS SERVER

Ma'am, I'm sorry. The day has come, you and your daughter have to leave. This house has been condemned. Here is the order. Ma'am, I'm sorry. The day has come...

THELMA

But where God, where. Where is next? What is next?

The Process Server turns and goes out the door.

Lights become brighter.

Christine pours a cup of coffee and gives it to Thelma.

CHRISTINE

Next is what, Mom.

Christine goes back to her room. The Process Server comes back through the door.

PROCESS SERVER

Ma'am, I'm sorry. The day has come...

THELMA

The house will go all unused after today. The house will die, same as Martin died and...

The Process Server comes back through the door.

PROCESS SERVER

Ma'am, I'm sorry. The day has come...

THELMA

Maybe Christine and I will get another day or two. Maybe,

PROCESS SERVER

No.

A red light begins to flash.

THELMA

What time is it? I don't want you to wake Christine. What's that?

Thelma goes to the door and opens it.

Bright red light flashes.

Thelma closes the door.

THELMA

What's that? That's outside! My God, what's outside?

PROCESS SERVER

Ma'am, I'm sorry but the day has come...

Loud knocking at the door.

SHERIFF

Sheriff!

Loud knock on the door.

SHERIFF

Thayer County Sheriff! Open up please! We have a warrant!

THELMA

No, no, no, this isn't real. They've been here before, why do they have to come here again?

SHERIFF

Thayer County Sheriff! Open up or we will force the door!

THELMA

No, no. You've already been here and told me Martin is dead. Why are you here?

SHERIFF

Sheriff, open the door!

THELMA

Why are you here? I need to know why you're here. You can't be here, you will wake my baby,

> Thelma steps toward the door, it burst open; Two sheriffs, one wielding a battering ram, force their way in. They both wear black. One has a clipboard of paperwork.

> PROJECTIONS dissolve from the slopes of Everest to mounds of trash stacked in a variety of dark plastic bags.

SHERIFF

Are you Thelma Zidar?

THELMA (BEWILDERED.)

Yes.

SHERIFF

We are here to enforce an order of eviction from Thayer County. Also, is there a Christine Zidar in the house?

THELMA

Yes.

SHERIFF

Where is she?

THELMA

She's in her bed.

SHERIFF

Where's her bedroom, Ma'am?

THELMA

Upstairs.

SHERIFF

We're here to arrest her for prostitution.

THELMA

What?

SHERIFF

I said,

THELMA

I know what you said but what does that mean?

SHERIFF

It means we're taking her in. Is she upstairs? God! My God. Look at this place.

The Sheriffs set off into the garbage towards Christine's room.

> Light fade up on the mounds of trash. The Sheriffs gaze in amazement. Thelma obstructs their way.

THELMA

What proof do you have? She can't be a prostitute she is just a baby, a baby sleeping in her crib,

> Thelma stands solidly in their way.

THELMA

No! No, no, no, you can't go up! You will wake the baby, with Martin there, with the baby.

SHERIFF 1

Baby? What baby? We're going up to arrest Christine Zidar, ma'am, what are you talking about? What baby? Who the hell is Martin? Some damned john of hers? She got a john in there too? Listen, let us by so we can go up and see. Come on, just let us by.

> They push past her.

THELMA

Christine! Christine!

SHERIFF 1

Don't interfere ma'am, don't interfere! We've got a warrant for her arrest!

> Thelma pushes ahead and stands in front of the closed door of Christine's room.

THELMA

No! No! You will leave her alone!

SHERIFF 2

Step aside…

> Sheriff 2 comes forward with the battering ram, pushes
> Thelma aside and knocks on the door.

SHERIFF 2

Sheriff! Christine Zidar, open up, we have a warrant for your arrest!

> Lights fade up in Christine's room.

> Christine sits up as Leandra snuggles up to her.

SHERIFF 1

Sheriff! Open up,

CHRISTINE

Lewis, why don't you just come in? Don't pretend to be the sheriff, what kind of game is this? Some big macho thing?

> PROJECTION OF LEWIS looking at Christine.

LEWIS' PROJECTION

This is your own fault Christine scaring me like you did with that business about Mount Everest and all the bodies on it and how morbid that is, Christine you should be ashamed of yourself thinking anybody wants to hear such stuff, you got me so shook up I forgot to call home and say I'd be pulling an overnight.

SHERIFF 1

Sheriff!

LEWIS' PROJECTION

My wife thinks I stayed out drunk all night because of you, She thinks I'm back off the wagon and it's your fault Christine!

Christine gets up, goes to the door and listens. Leandra pulls the sheet up around her neck.

LEANDRA

He isn't going to go away.

SHERIFF 1

Sheriff!

CHRISTINE

That's Tanady, I can hear Tanady's voice, Leandra

Tanady's voice filter's through the wall.

TANADY'S VOICE

Christine Zidar! Open up!

Christine jumps back into bed, next to Leandra.

Tanady's Projection (or Tanady live) appears, looking down on the action.

CHRISTINE

Hey Tanady, who are you going to be today, and who is pretending to be you today Tanady, a rapist and then you'll want to do it to me, is that how you'll get your rocks off this time?

TANADYS PROJECTION

Oh no Christine, I'm going to bust into this room and you will be very sorry you gave me that "being somebody else" routine. What kind of damned problem do you have Christine, what the hell is the matter with you?

Christine sits up in bed. Leandra covers up.

CHRISTINE

I know it's you, Tanady! The disguises don't fool me.

Tanady's Projection fades out.

SHERIFF

Sheriff! Open up we know you're in there,

Christine looks around beginning to panic. She focuses on a point on the slopes of Mt. Everest.

Serdon's Projection fades up.

CHRISTINE

This is our room, you can't come in here.

SERDON'S PROJECTION

You're crazy Christine, you know that?

CHRISTINE

Serdon! Serdon, if it isn't Lewis or Tanady it must be you Serdon, who are you going to pretend to be today? Three Nuns again?

SERDON'S PROJECTION

Christine you drive me crazy. You've got to stop saying crazy things, being a good fuck isn't enough, you've got to try and be normal, like everybody else Christine. Don't be crazy!

CHRISTINE

You're not fooling me!

Serdon's Projection fades out.

SHERIFF

Open up, God damn it you're under arrest, we'll break down the door!

Barry's Projection fades up.

Christine gets up, goes to the window and gazes out.

CHRISTINE

Not today, Barry!

BARRY'S PROJECTION

Damn you! You ruined me Christine, you deserve to be arrested for what you do, yes you ruined me, what you do is against the law after all, you know,

> Leandra suddenly sits up, eyes wide open.

> Sound of a loud knock at the door.

SHERIFF 1

Christine Zidar, open up. One last chance before we break the door. Open up, Christine!

> Christine looks over to the door. Leandra follows her gaze, then joins Christine at the window.

> Projections of all the johns fade up.

CHRISTINE

Where do we go?

TANADY'S PROJECTION

Put her in custody!

LEWIS' PROJECTION

Put her in handcuffs,

CHRISTINE/LEANDRA

I can hear your voices, I know who you are.

TANADY'S PROJECTION

When you look in the mirror what you see is yourself.

SERDON'S PROJECTION

You might not like what you see but that is you.

CHRISTINE (TO LEANDRA.)

Before we were born there was nothing, wonderful nothing, like death must actually be; all those bodies just lying there in nothingness.

CHRISTINE/LEANDRA

She's always known how she would end up, it was inevitable. She'd always known it was there, where it was.

MACK'S PROJECTION

Break it down.

LEANDRA

Knowing that if there was a God he would never allow it to happen.

Christine puts her arms around Leandra and kisses her.

CHRISTINE

Why did we come here?

Leandra puts her arms around Christine and hugs her.

LEANDRA

This is where there was.

Sound of the battering ram smashing against the door once.

Christine opens the window

Projections of the windswept slopes of Mt. Everest; stark, plumes of snow rise among the dead bodies and cairns. The SOUND of wind comes through the window.

Christine and Leandra step outside the window.

SHERIFF 1 VOICE

Break it in!

Sound of the battering ram hitting and splintering the doorframe

SHERRIF'S 1 and 2 burst through the door.

SHERIFF 1

Stop!

Christine and Leandra leap from the window.

Projections of all her johns' turning and watching them fall. They turn away one by one dissolving to the empty slopes, wind whipping the frozen dead bodies of Mt. Everest.

Projection of Christine and Leandra, in white nightgowns, arms around each other's shoulders, walking away into the blinding snow, disappearing in the whiteness.

Projection of the summit of Mt. Everest glowing brightly. A wisp of snow flashes up and freezes at the center of the peak. Fade out.

THE END

Acknowledgements

The playwright would like to thank Kit Patrick Corson and Sharon Roberts for providing a sojourn in the Sonora Desert, G.G. Hale for taking time from her own series of books to read and offer comments, novelist Jim Meirose for his outstanding novel, editor Charlie Franco for his dedication and insight, and Jennifer Rebecca Bailey for her invaluable input.

Richard S. Bailey is the recipient of numerous press awards for writing, directing, producing, acting and designing theatre in the United States and Europe. His published plays include a deconstruction of the Antigone myth, *Tiresias Lies: The Insidious Plot of the Men with No Left Shoe*; a sci-fi excursion into the story of Abraham and Isaac with an extended introductory monologue, *Deus Ex Machina and The Hands of the Beholder*, which was produced to excellent press in Los Angeles and Berkeley; *Window Pieces: A Collection of Reflections and Points of View*; and two volumes of *Children's Theatre Story Books*. His yet to be published translation of *Growing Absurd: Six Short Plays by Jean Tardieu*, the first of the seminal absurdist's works to be translated into the American genre, has been performed and is being studied in American colleges and universities. He was personally invited to work with Nobel Laureate Samuel Beckett at the West Berlin Academy of Art in 1977. At Beckett's request, he waited thirty years before performing *Krapp's Last Tape* as part of his production of *Shuffle, Shuffle, Step: Three Short Plays by Samuel Beckett*, in Los Angeles, 2007. He is a former Associate Director of the Los Angeles Theatre Center and Los Angeles Actors' Theatre, Producing Director of the San Quentin Drama Workshop, and Producer of the feature film *Cock & Bull Story*, based on the British play. His comic, scifi novel *Off On A Tangent* is currently available online.